CAMBRIDGE LIBRARY COLLECTION

Books of enduring scholarly value

History

The books reissued in this series include accounts of historical events and movements by eye-witnesses and contemporaries, as well as landmark studies that assembled significant source materials or developed new historiographical methods. The series includes work in social, political and military history on a wide range of periods and regions, giving modern scholars ready access to influential publications of the past.

Testimonies Concerning Slavery

Moncure Conway (1832–1907) was born on his family's plantation in Virginia, but became a committed abolitionist soon after he left college. He joined abolitionist rallies and moved from Methodism to the Unitarian ministry, eventually becoming a freethinker. Conway became increasingly isolated from his family as a result of his abolitionist activism, his marriage to an abolitionist, and the resettling of a group of his father's escaped slaves in Ohio during the civil war. This book was published in 1865, soon after moved to Britain, where he lived for over 30 years, became a supporter of women's suffrage, and moved in the same intellectual circles as Dickens, Carlyle, Lyell and Darwin. His description of the injustices of slavery, including the slave trading in the southern plantations that triggered the secession of southern states and the civil war, is set in the context of his personal experiences and his evolving ethical views.

T0370588

Cambridge University Press has long been a pioneer in the reissuing of out-of-print titles from its own backlist, producing digital reprints of books that are still sought after by scholars and students but could not be reprinted economically using traditional technology. The Cambridge Library Collection extends this activity to a wider range of books which are still of importance to researchers and professionals, either for the source material they contain, or as landmarks in the history of their academic discipline.

Drawing from the world-renowned collections in the Cambridge University Library, and guided by the advice of experts in each subject area, Cambridge University Press is using state-of-the-art scanning machines in its own Printing House to capture the content of each book selected for inclusion. The files are processed to give a consistently clear, crisp image, and the books finished to the high quality standard for which the Press is recognised around the world. The latest print-on-demand technology ensures that the books will remain available indefinitely, and that orders for single or multiple copies can quickly be supplied.

The Cambridge Library Collection will bring back to life books of enduring scholarly value (including out-of-copyright works originally issued by other publishers) across a wide range of disciplines in the humanities and social sciences and in science and technology.

Testimonies Concerning Slavery

MONCURE DANIEL CONWAY

CAMBRIDGE
UNIVERSITY PRESS

CAMBRIDGE UNIVERSITY PRESS

Cambridge, New York, Melbourne, Madrid, Cape Town, Singapore,
São Paolo, Delhi, Dubai, Tokyo, Mexico City

Published in the United States of America by Cambridge University Press, New York

www.cambridge.org
Information on this title: www.cambridge.org/9781108026246

This edition first published 1855
This digitally printed version 2010

ISBN 978-1-108-02624-6 Paperback

TESTIMONIES

CONCERNING

S L A V E R Y.

By M. D. CONWAY,

A NATIVE OF VIRGINIA.

SECOND EDITION.

LONDON:

CHAPMAN AND HALL, 193 PICCADILLY.

MDCCCLXV.

THIS LITTLE BOOK,

WRITTEN IN THE INTEREST OF SIMPLE JUSTICE, CAN BEAR NO NAME
MORE FITLY THAN THAT OF ONE WHOSE LOYALTY TO EVERY
JUST CAUSE HAS NEVER BEEN FOUND WANTING :

TO

PETER ALFRED TAYLOR, M.P.

IT IS THEREFORE INSCRIBED BY ONE WHO, ADMIRING HIM AS A PUBLIC
MAN, IS NOT UNMINDFUL OF PRIVATE FRIENDSHIP.

CONTENTS.

INTRODUCTORY NOTE.

It is with the hope that the testimony of one who has passed twenty-three years in the Slave States may contribute something toward that healthier public opinion which is necessary to a right dealing with the issues which must be perpetually evolved in the struggle between Slavery and Freedom, that I take the stand as a witness. The revolution which the experiences herein related gradually wrought in my own convictions and life, against the persuasion of every natural tie, inspires my chief confidence that they will have weight with other minds. I do not pretend to give any complete view of Slavery, the worst phases of which — as those of the plantations of the far South—I have never seen; I give only a few sketches from a region where Slavery exists in its mildest form, and where it has been less regarded and studied.

I have long believed that the friends of Liberty can help America much more by rekindling their old watch-fires, which sadly need fuel, than by advocating this or that measure or man that may be for the time associated with the struggle. What America needs now is not a sultry indulgence, but a bracing criticism, always supposing that criticism to be made in the interest of Liberty and not of Slavery. It is related that, at the Federal repulse at Charleston, a Negro who bore the flag crawled a long distance amid a storm of shot and shell, dragging his wounded body, but still holding up the flag. When he regained his companions, his only words were, " I did not let it (the flag) touch the ground once." Let the voices of all true men keep it ever before the rulers of America, that her banner is far nobler so long as a Negro holds it up with devotion, as too pure to touch the ground, than if it should wave over every fort and city of the South tainted with compromise or soiled with Slavery.

TESTIMONIES CONCERNING SLAVERY.

CHAPTER I.

Early recollections—Slavery and the household—Negro characteristics—Fate of a Negro genius.

THE town of Falmouth, in Virginia, on the Rappahannock river, has been associated with important military
events during the present war.   Before the war, it was
a village of about a thousand inhabitants, all of whom
were very poor, with the exception of five or six families
which were very rich.   It is quite an ancient place, and
was originally inhabited by some Scotchmen,—amongst
others, an uncle of the poet Campbell,—who made it a
centre of trade between the rich uplands of Virginia and
Baltimore.   It was once the exact head of navigation
on the Rappahannock ; but afterwards the river was so
filled with bars, that the trade fell to Fredericksburg,
about two miles lower.   Falmouth has the advantage of
being close to the falls which furnish the most magnificent water-power in Virginia ; and if that State had
been free, it must have been one of the chief manufac-
turing towns in America.

It was near this village that I was born, and in
it that my parents resided during nearly all the early
years that I can remember.   There were a great many
slaves and free Negroes in the neighbourhood.   My
father then owned fifty or sixty slaves, and many of my

B

relatives a larger number. My parents were very kind
to their slaves; and, indeed, I think that the marked
contrast between the treatment of slaves to which I had
been accustomed at home and that which I witnessed
elsewhere, was the first occasion of my attention being
drawn to what was going on around me. And yet no
amount of benevolent intentions, or watchfulness, or
religious observances on their part, was adequate to
secure a quiet or happy home. Not long ago, in conversation with a strong defender of Negro Slavery, I
found that the corner-stone of his theory was an impression that there was in the homestead of the South a simplicity, a patriarchal relationship between the servants
and superiors, which contrasted favourably with the corresponding conditions in other communities, where, he
maintained, the relation between servant and master
being purely and at each moment mercenary, the ties
must be galling to both parties. I can well believe
that a scholar who had never come into personal contact with Slavery, might think of that system as wearing
in America the Oriental costume of customs and relations
which it wore in the early days when slaves belonged to
and loved men who had ransomed them from death as
captives, or with races and ages under less pressure than
our own to turn every thing to gold. In Brazil, where
Slavery exists in connection with a race and government
far behind any that it can find in the United States, it
is less out of place, and need not use so much violence
and coercion to exist at all; and hence there is much
more simplicity and repose there with the institution.
And so I was obliged to assure the gentleman alluded to
that, however coarse and hard the relation between servants and employers in free communities might be, he
was, in looking to the Southern States, appealing to an
absolutely mythical Arcadia. Few are the really peace-

ful days that I remember as having smiled on my old
Virginian home; the outbreaks of the Negroes among
themselves, the disobediences which the necessary discipline can never suffer to be overlooked, the terrors of
devoted parents at the opportunities for the display of
evil tempers and the inception of nameless vices among
their sons, I remember as the demons haunting those
days.   And for these most painful circumstances, giving
to nearly every day its " scene," there is no compensation in the work accomplished.   With two Irish girls
for servants in Ohio, I am quite sure that I have had
more work done, and infinitely better done, and with far
less interruption of domestic quiet, than my father ever
got from all his slaves.   No doubt, if he had availed
himself of the severe methods used by others around
him, he might have got more work and money out of
his slaves; for only perpetual violence and sleepless suspicion can really get any thing like the full amount of
work out of men and women who know only the curse,
and none of the rewards, of toil.   I have often heard my
parents say that the care of slaves had made them pre-
maturely old.

The impression has gone around the world with
ubiquitous sable minstrels that the slaves are a merry,
singing, dancing population, far removed from the cares
that gnaw the hearts of more civilised classes.   In all
the twenty-three years of my life in the land of Slavery,
I never saw a Negro-dance, though in those years I
have heard of a few in our neighbourhood.   The slaves
of the Border States are almost invariably members of
the Baptist and Methodist societies, which are particularly rigid in denying them such amusements.   On the
large plantations of the far South, dances are encouraged,
and formerly were frequent; but of late years they have
become infrequent, through the all-absorbing tendencies

of the Negroes toward religious meetings.   My observation confirms that of Dr. Russell when he visited the South as correspondent of the London *Times*, that the Negroes are a notably melancholy people.   I have rarely known their enthusiasm enlisted in any thing except prayer - and - experience meetings and funerals. Our own kitchen-fireside was nightly the scene of religious exercises and conversations which were very fascinating to me, and from which I had to be dragged with each returning bed - time.   The dreams, visions, and ecstasies there related were as gorgeous as those of the *Pilgrim's Progress ;* for these humble and ignorant souls, denied the reading of the Bible, had conceived a symbolism of their own, and burdens of prophecy, and had changed the fields on which they toiled into the pavements of the New Jerusalem, glorified with spirits arrayed in white.   The cant phrases of the white preachers whom they listened to had become alive to them, and mingled strangely in their speech and hymns ; they had, too, their own rudimental Swedenborgianism and Transcendentalism.

A boy was born on my father's estate, who was named Charles.   His obvious parents were servants, whom my father had long owned; but they were both quite black, and the boy was nearly white, besides being embarrassingly like a pious gentleman who now and then visited us.   This lad at an early age indicated a remarkable intelligence, and was also of a remarkable beauty according to the European type.   As he grew older, he increased in vivacity, wit, and amiability; and at his sixteenth year I remember him as one of the handsomest and noblest specimens of Humanity.   Wherever he went in the village, a group of admiring white boys was around him, listening to his bewitching songs or romances or mimicries.   He seemed to us all a hero

of romance, and such a thing as remembering his colour
never entered our heads.

His occupation at this age was to attend my brother
and myself to and from our school, which was two miles
distant. The monotony of this daily journey he varied
by his songs and stories, and to him we both looked with
implicit reverence. He was active and brave too, proud
of being our protector, and eager to pounce upon the
biggest snake in our path, or encounter and subdue the
fiercest dog.

The day came to him, as it had to come to millions
before him, when he desired to learn what we were
learning in school. But the laws forbid the teaching
of a Negro to read under severest penalties ; and no
law relating to Negroes is so carefully and strictly enforced in the South as that which forbids their being
taught. The long imprisonment of Mrs. Douglas at
Norfolk, a few years ago, for teaching a Negro child
to read is a familiar case. In Falmouth, two or three
ladies whom I knew met on Sunday afternoon to teach
some Negro children ; they had not so met three times,
before they were dispersed by the authorities, although
it appeared that they only gave the children oral and
religious instruction. I do not believe that my father
approved these laws ; but being a justice of the county,
he of course must take care that the laws were observed
in his own house. So Charles's thirst must go unslaked.

There is a cruel pang that comes to nearly every
slave's life, which has been very little considered. It is
customary in nearly all households in the South for the
white and black children connected with each to play
together. The trial I have referred to comes when the
young Negroes who have hitherto been on this democratic footing with the young whites are presently de-
serted by their more fortunate companions, who enter

upon school-life and the acquaintance of white boys, and, ceasing to associate with their swarthy comrades any longer, meet them in future with the air of the master. This is the dawn of the first bitter consciousness of being a slave; and nothing can be sadder than to see the poor little things wandering about companionless and comfortless. It is doubtful whether either my brother or myself had natural gifts equal to the slaveboy Charles; nevertheless we were carried past him, and abandoned him. His knowledge, which once seemed to us unlimited, we gradually discovered to be inferior to our own. We gained new (white) companions, and should have been ashamed to be seen playing at any game with Charles.

But meanwhile the power of intellect and temperament which Nature had lodged in that youth increased. Had there been about him a society able to enclose that power in a fit engine, and set it upon true grooves, he might have borne the burdens which such souls are sent into the world to bear. But as it was, this power was as so much steam without a valve: it was a danger. His temper, from being mild, became bitter; his bravery became fierceness; and by his recklessness the whole family was kept in perpetual panic. Punishment only made him defiant. He was to be a noted personage in one way or another; his daring and ingenious tricks became at first the town's talk and then the town's alarm. He signalised his nineteenth year by setting fire to a house; whereupon my father was forced by public opinion, or perhaps by a legal order, to sell him to the far South. So Charles is now buried, alive or dead, among the cotton plantations.

Although I have dwelt upon this case because it is that which represents, in my own experience, one of the most tragical forms in which Slavery outrages human nature, yet let none think of this as an incident in any respect peculiar. On the contrary, I have myself known many cases where minds of high gifts have been thus waylaid and robbed of their God-given treasures by Slavery. It perhaps requires powers higher than any ordinarily vouchsafed to the Anglo-Saxon to discern the rare quality of the purely Negro spirit and mind; but, were we to grant all that Cant and Sophistry say about the inferiority of the Negro, what shall be said of those millions of the Southern slaves who have Anglo-Saxon blood in them? Not one-third of the Southern slaves are purely African; and in at least a third of them the white blood predominates. Certainly these are not under the curse of Ham. At least we can be certain that the pride, the curiosity, the thirst for knowledge, which are inherent in the blood of the white race, must render Slavery to these a fearful crucifixion. Had Charles been born in the North, I know he would have been a noble and a distinguished man. And I have known at least ten others in Virginia who, I am persuaded, would, by a few years' tuition of freedom, have been equal in character and influence to Douglass, Charles Remond, and others.

I know that there is an impression abroad that the people of mixed blood in the Southern States are a very low and vicious class,—an impression which naturally originated with the slaveholders, to whom coloured people are always odious and evil in proportion as they are hard to keep enslaved. My observation leads me to believe that, so far from being a poor or inferior set, we might, under proper training, have had from just that mixture of the Saxon mind with the African tempera- ment some of the first men of the world. They are said to have bad health: it proves only the greater chafing of the yoke, and the intentional severity with which it is made to weigh upon them. They are driven to the lowest occupations.

But the laws of God are inviolable. The South has by its own passions forged, and given a Saxon temper to, the sword which is now suspended over it, and which must soon fall. For these are not the men who run off at once to the Union lines; they remain to strike the blow for their race, and share the fate of comrades. They are such as Denmark Vesey, who travelled through the world with his master, and might have had freedom a thousand times; but returned to South Carolina, to set on foot a gigantic plot for insurrection. A group of such I met from the cotton plantations early in this war; they had made their way to Ohio to consult with Abolitionists; having done so, they abandoned the free soil upon which they stood and went back to the far South, to abide their time with the rest. And there are thousands of these who have long lived in the North, and whose motto is now SOUTHWARD: in them are the fiery hearts of crusaders who march to rescue the holy places of Humanity from the tread of the infidel. And for them wait the multitudes of starved intellects, beggared hearts, and famished souls, who have long lain under the altar, and cried day and night, " How long, O Lord; how long!"

CHAPTER II.

Treatment of slaves—A Virginian legislator.

I HAVE often heard it assumed that the interest of a man in his property is sufficient to protect the slaves from cruel treatment. All animals belonging to the uses of civilised life are property; and yet societies for the prevention of cruelty to them are found necessary. The assumption is, that the love of property is the strongest human feeling, and can check all other passions; and yet history is perpetually showing that the masses of men have been always sacrificing property to superstition, fear, lust, and anger. In the case of the slaves, one frequently observes in the heads of families the same cautious disposition to protect their slaves from injury, that may be observed elsewhere with regard to the money or estate which are the results of years of economy and toil. But the younger persons of the household have no such associations with the slaves, and are willing to sacrifice their well-being to pride or passion. And where there arises between the young master and the slave any conflict, of course it would be disastrous to humiliate the white before the black to the slightest extent. However much the older heads may deplore the collision, discipline requires that every threat or sentence which a hot-headed boy may make shall be executed; since he is to be trained, not to be the equal of the slaves, but their master.

My observation leads me to believe that kindness to the slaves is rather the exception than the rule. And I have been accustomed to trace this fact to the necessi-

ties of the institution itself.   A dumb beast is much less
apt to rouse anger than a slave: the slave can be defiant, sulky, or angry.   This, where the obedience of an
animal can be claimed, excites the master to fury: and
this fury is reinforced by the fact, that if the slightest
defiance or disobedience is passed over, there is danger
that the general discipline of the estate may be impaired.
So far from a man's interest in his slave as property
being a guarantee against the laceration of that slave,
such laceration may be, and frequently is, the only
means of retaining him as property.   "Breaking their
spirit" is a phrase as frequently used with regard to
slaves as to horses.   Sometimes a slave must be killed,
that the mastery of a hundred others may be secured.
No large body of slaves could be held securely, unless it
was understood that there would be no hesitation in
shooting any who should rebel.

My belief is, that there is an element in the constitution of the Anglo-Saxon man which, though contribut-
ing much to his power when under the proper restraints,
does, when not so restrained, render him particularly
cruel to those under him.   *Anglo* is derived from *ang*, a
hook, and *Saxon* from *sax*, a dagger ; and though centuries have transmuted to power the natural ferocity
which originated his name, the Anglo-Saxon can easily
be reduced to a hard and cruel personage ; it being also
proverbial that the best when corrupted is the worst.
I have conversed with many intelligent Negroes who
have known Slavery under Spanish and French masters,
and they have assured me that under them the cruelties
of our Southern plantations are rare.   It is well known
that under the predominance of French influence at
New Orleans, Slavery, though as licentious and cor-
rupting as elsewhere, is not at all so inhuman as in
other regions of the Southern States.   The crowds that

can stand without wincing and see two men mutilate each other in the brutal London prize-fight, indicate the presence of a vein of brutality which it would not do to trust with unlimited power. I have observed that the most polished Southern gentleman is transformed, when even a slight collision between him and his slave occurs, into a pitiless and formidable animal; and know that his complete power over another's body and soul keeps alive, even if generally asleep, a demon in his breast which civilisation has nearly exorcised in England and the Free States, so far as the man of the same class of society is concerned.

The cowhide embodies the only theory of punishment recognised by the slave-system. And one of the worst effects of its constant use is, that it furnishes the slaves themselves with their only idea of punishing their own children. They too are trained to cruelty and brutality, and are too apt to imitate the barbarity of the overseer in their own cabins. From all these circumstances, cruelty has become the law of Southern society; and I believe that it would be difficult to find a slave without a serious scar.

No doubt there are many humane and tender-hearted persons in the South; but the law gives the widest license to those who are not such. And a bad law can demoralise a community far more than a good man or woman can moralise them. There is no passion so vile, no disposition so cruel, but it may spend its fullest fury under the cover of law. The law always presumes the slave to be in the wrong; and his inability to give testimony against his master is the only element required for an absolutely despotic rule. The fact that this is the law destroys the only shelter the slave might otherwise have,—public opinion.

Near my father's estate was one owned by a certain

" captain," who was one of the worst of men, and who had a face naturally belonging to the worst of men. This man was known to have killed one of his slaves in the most cold-blooded manner, having beaten him to death in the sight of several other slaves. The murder was generally known, and I never heard of its being denied by the murderer; but only his slaves had witnessed it,—and that was the same as if so many oxen had witnessed it,—consequently there was not even a coroner's inquest held.

Not long after this the same man brought three or four women to the county-court of Stafford, charging them with having conspired to poison him. The jury decided that there was not the slightest evidence to show that the women had made any such attempt. The general opinion amongst those present at the trial was, that either the captain knew he deserved to be poisoned by them, and was really alarmed; or that the women being, on account of their age and delicacy, not very marketable, the captain wished the county to hang them, that he might get the money which the State paid the owner for every slave it destroyed.

As large a crowd had gathered about the doors as was usual on court-days, and they looked with eager interest upon the captain when he left the court-room with the three Negro women,—one of whom was aged, and the other two in quite feeble health. I remember well how the man's face was flushed with a sense of his power over these women,—a power unlimited by any law. Glancing triumphantly at the crowd, he took the women to a cart in which they had been brought to the court-house; there he bound their ankles and wrists, and bound them to each other; then, after displaying six raw-hides,—whips compared with which the cat-o'-nine-tails is merciful,—he tore down the dresses from their shoulders and backs, and ordering the driver, husband of one of the women, to drive homeward, began to beat and lacerate the backs of these women frightfully. The crowd stood witnessing all this with a mere curiosity, watching the cart as it went on its way with its tragical freight; and, after it had disappeared, the brute still sent back to our ears the pæans of his triumph in the shrieks of the tortured and imploring wretches who had never wronged him.

There were doubtless many in the vast crowd who recoiled at this sight; some who muttered that it was an " infernal shame." But the essence of the tragedy was, that any interference with the scoundrel would have been illegal—that the law was all on his side. And the ultimate effect of it all was to harden the people and demoralise the humane : the whole scene passed from their remembrance with the next trial in the court-room.

I lived in Stafford County long enough to see that " captain" elected twice to represent that county in the Legislature of Virginia, and each time over one of the humanest and ablest men in the community. He now occupies, as I have heard, a high position in the Confederate army.

CHAPTER III.

The slave-whipper—Nemesis.

To get a farm cultivated, or a large amount of work done, with such low wages as a half-dollar a year spent in twisted cowhides, is a temptation which the lower nature can scarcely resist where it has the power. The sad scenes enacted in England when a sailor or soldier is flogged have raised an important party, anxious for the abolition of the custom, as it has been abolished in France and America; but it must be remembered that in the Southern States such scenes are normal, the lash being the only incentive to labour. The political economy of the South accepts this as the relation between capital and labour. When Slavery established itself lately in the territory of New Mexico,—wrested from its grasp by the last Congress, with all other territories of the United States,—it announced the right of the lash, not only between master and slave, but employer and white *employé*. By an act of January 1859 peonage was established in New Mexico, the fourth section of which prohibited courts from taking cognisance of correction inflicted by a master upon his servants; "for," it says, "they are considered domestic servants to their masters, and they should correct their neglects and faults; for as soldiers are punished by their chiefs, without the intervention of the civil authority, by reason of the salary they enjoy, an equal right should be granted those persons who pay their money to be served in the protection of their property."

On the farms and plantations the Negroes are lashed

by an overseer, or by a slave under his supervision ; a special room for punishment being a concomitant of every homestead. If the slave resists, it is an offence severely punishable ; and to kill a slave in the act of re- sistance is legal. Such resistance is therefore very rare.

In the towns and villages the flogging is done by a special and legally-appointed functionary. It is only under severe emergencies or in the heat of passion that gentlemen and ladies beat their own slaves. The gentle- men shun it as a temporary descent to the social grade of the overseer or the constable, as the slave-whipper is called, and the ladies have too much sensibility to inflict complete chastisement ; so they merely write on a bit of note-paper, " Mr. ———, will you give Negro-girl Nancy ——— lashes, and charge to account." Nancy, with swimming eyes, waits at the door whilst Madame Serena writes this ; takes the billet to the constable's door ; waits with a group of boys or coarse young men around her, some of whom jeer at her as one who is " going to catch it," others of whom stand with silent curiosity watching her falling tears, until the grim man of fate appears, leads her in, and locks the door in the face of the idle crowd.

I remember no building in our village so well as the slave-whipper's old, prison-like quarters, built of brick and limestone ; and I recall vividly the fascination it had for myself and the other boys. It was known as " Captain Pickett's." The captain himself, with his hard, stony look, and his iron-gray hair and beard, was the very animal to inhabit such a shell, and seemed to me always as a bit of his own grim house that had taken to walking on the street. I never remember to have seen him elsewhere than walking up and down before the door of his mysterious building ; and never heard a word fall from his thin, compressed lips. It

was plain that he felt the shadow over him; for the
characters who do the necessary but cruel work of
Slavery are not pleasantly received by those who employ them. Captain Pickett had no personal connection
with the "society" of which he was a most important
adjunct; and his children, when their mother was dead
and they grew old enough to enter society, abandoned,
one by one, their native village, and were scarcely
heard of again, so far did they remove from the shadow
of the old man's den; and he, grim and solitary, must
often have felt that the pangs we inflict, no less than the
kindnesses rendered, are returned to our bosoms, heaped
up and shaken together.

The respectable family-heads of Falmouth were
always particularly strict and careful in forbidding their
children any play or loitering in the neighbourhood of
Captain Pickett's; and to such prohibited places the
eager feet and wide-open eyes of boyhood are as faithful
as the needle to the pole. About this particular building we lingered and peered with an insatiable curiosity,
all the more pertinaciously for being so often driven or
dragged away. And our curiosity found enough fuel to
keep it inflamed; for few hours ever passed without
bringing some victim to his door. At this business the
captain made his living; and it was by no means dull:
he held open accounts with nearly every family in the
neighbourhood. Around each victim we crowded, and
when he or she disappeared and the door was shut, we
—the boys—would rush around to all the walls, crevices,
and backyards which we knew so well, gaining many
a point from which we could see the half-naked cower-
ing slave and the falling lash, and hear, with short-lived
awe, the blows and the imploring tones, swelling to cries
as the flogging proceeded.

Perhaps at that moment some tourist from Old or

New England, travelling through the South to ascertain
" the facts" about Slavery, is at the hospitable board of
the writhing slave's owner, learning how merciful the
treatment of the slave is.   He will write in his Diary,
that, during several weeks passed at the residence of this
or that large slaveholder, he saw no cases of severe
punishment, though he observed keenly.   He does not
know to this day, perhaps, that in every Southern community there is a " Captain Pickett's place,"—a dark
and unrevealed closet, connected by blind ways with the
elegant mansions.   His Diary might have had a different entry had he consulted the slaves or the boys.   I
have not been careful to defend myself from the charge
of hard-heartedness, in that I could, as a boy, seek out
and behold without any memorable horror the scenes I
have described : the atmosphere around me was not one
of any horror at these things.   I remember very well
that the tenderness which I, and I believe all other children, felt in early childhood for the Negroes — quite
equal in some cases to that felt for our own parents—
was considered " babyish" among the boys whom we
met in our first ventures on the street ; whilst the more
advanced boys regarded a domineering tone toward Negroes as " manly."   Such aspirations in the young indicate sufficiently what is the fashion among their elders.
Moreover, the necessary alternative of not preventing or
protesting against a wrong is to become insensible to it.

The slave-whipper is well paid for his ugly work,
and makes a " handsome living."   But the silent old
man of whom I have been writing came at last to pre-
fer no living at all to such a one ; for one day a sobbing
girl, bearing in her hand an order for forty lashes, was
unable to gain admittance ; whereupon the neighbours
broke down the door, and found that Captain Pickett
had hung himself by the side of his own whipping-post.

He had, at least, that sombre grace of Judas; and I have some hope, since finding that his work was odious to him, that, in the lonely den where he stood face to face with Humanity and God, many a blow written in the bond may have been spared.

The ancient village has, by the devastations of war, been almost obliterated from the earth. The last tidings I had of the grim building, it was a storehouse for Federal bombshells. A glimpse I once had of the old man, with lash lifted over the tender form of a young girl, abided in my memory; until of late the view has dissolved into the figure of Nemesis, standing with uplifted scourge upon that same spot, where it must stand until every groan wrung from a black breast shall find its echo in a white one.

CHAPTER IV.

The slave harvest— Mysteries of a shamble.

I AM strongly inclined to believe that, if it should be settled that Slavery is to continue, it would be for the interest of humanity that the African slave-trade should be reopened. Those of the Southern States who have argued in favour of importing slaves from Africa have certainly not been the most selfish or brutal portion of their communities ; but they have reasoned, not groundlessly, that the steady supply of Southern plantations from the slave-breeding States involves far worse evils than the African trade would, if conducted under legal sanction. The African trade, they allege, if made legal, would no longer be driven to use insecure or small ships, but would find its interest in having commodious and healthy arrangements ; and by them the Negroes would be removed from barbarism. By the inter-state slave-trade, families, with more distinctly-formed ties, are broken up annually, and the Negroes are taken from regions of greater to those of lesser enlightenment. I certainly have never been able to compare the physical sufferings of the African trade as I have read of them, with the fearful agonies which I have witnessed as attendant on the making up, in Virginia, of gangs for the Southern markets.

Not more regularly does the farmer put in his scythe to reap his annual harvest, than the slave-dealer visits the estates around him to gather up those who are ripe for sale. Every slave-mother trains her child from in-

fancy with the full knowledge that, the more perfect
the growth of her child, the more certainly will it be
selected for the gang.   In the Border States, where
there are few large plantations, it is of course necessary
that the increase of the slaves over the small number requisite for household use shall be sold, otherwise each is
but another mouth to be fed and back to be clothed.   If
any one is too conscientious to sell slaves, he must cease
to own them, or they will keep him poor.   As a general
thing, the chief pecuniary resource in the Border States
is the breeding of slaves ; and I grieve to say that there
is too much ground for the charges that general licentiousness among the slaves, for the purpose of a large increase,
is compelled by some masters and encouraged by mány.
The period of maternity is hastened, the average youth
of Negro mothers being nearly three years earlier than
that of any free race, and an old maid is utterly unknown
among the women.   Against this systematic corruption
there must be many inward revolts among Southerners ;
but where laws are made for the inhuman, the human
are apt to be silent.   I remember having heard a conversation between a Methodist preacher of the Baltimore
Conference and a worthy member of the circuit over
which he presided in Virginia.   This preacher found,
upon his arrival, that several prominent members of the
society were actually encouraging the usual wholesale
prostitution on their estates for mercenary ends, and was
in great trouble as to the course he should pursue.   He
had asked advice from this his most blameless brother,
and this was the reply (given with a deep sigh) which
he—and I—heard : " It is impossible to even agitate
this matter in any Church in this State without ruining
that Church."

Up to this day not one of those Southern clergymen
who lately made their appeal for sympathy to the civi-

lised world has ever protested against this horrible corruption.

Nothing can be sadder than the scene in any household or in any " quarters" when the well-known dealer
appears. As a hen gathers her chickens when the hawk
is seen, so do the slave-mothers gather their little ones,
whilst fruitless efforts are made to get the elder ones—
those likely to be sold—out of the way, or to hide them.
From under beds and from closets and boxes they are
dragged, and priced before their parents' eyes.   It is
decided that Mary is not full grown yet—she may stay
six months longer ; but John is ready and ripe—he
must go.   It were vain to attempt to portray the agonies
of these cruel bargains, as the dealer goes from house to
house plucking the flower of every flock.

Perhaps nothing that I could report from my own
observation would give my reader so vivid a perception
of the barter in human beings as some quotations which
I shall make from a package of letters which fell into my
hands about two years ago, and which I labelled *Mysteries
of the Shamble*.

The firm of Kephart and Co., Alexandria, Virginia,
was, ever since I can remember, the chief slave-dealing
firm in that State, and perhaps any where along the
border between the Free and Slave States.   Every slave
that tries to escape to a Free State was invariably sold if
caught, and generally lodged in Kephart's shamble, and
never suffered to return to the place from which he ran,
lest he should tell others the means of his escape.   The
proximity of Alexandria to Maryland, in many portions
of which slaves were valueless except for sale, brought
him the trade of that State.

Upon the secession of Virginia, the United States
made a successful effort to occupy Alexandria.   One of
the first spots visited by our troops was the shamble of

Kephart and Co.   The firm had fled, and taken its sale-
able articles with it; but a single one remained—an old
man, chained to the middle of the floor by the leg.   He
was released, and the ring and chain which bound him
sent to the Rev. Henry Ward Beecher. A friend of mine
among the soldiers present filled his pockets with letters
and papers which were found strewn about the floor of
the office adjoining.   These fell into my hands.   They
consist of bills of sale, lists of Negroes on various estates
ready for purchase, and others who would be ready
the next year.   The letters show that the firm was in
correspondence with the most eminent families of that
region.   From these I select some from which to give
literal and characteristic extracts.

No. 1 is from a Mr. Bacon Tait, who seems to have
represented the higher branches of the trade at Richmond,
Virginia.   After giving account of certain sales, this
gentleman has the following Baconian reflections: " Mr.
Boudor complains a good deal about the Negroes he has
for sale, and I acknowledge that he has sufficient cause.
It was, all in all, a most wretched lot of Negroes when I
saw them, and it was perhaps false in me for not advising
the sale here of at least three-quarters of them.   I assure
you, captain, that inferior Negroes are never cheap for
the *Louisiana* market.   Trash and defective are never
permanently profitable.   They are very frequently sold at
a profit for the time being ; yet the sales as often recoil
upon the vendor, with detriment more than counter-
balancing such profit."

In No. 2 appears some lineament of the Mr. Boudor
alluded to in the foregoing letter.   In New Orleans,
from which he writes, Mr. Boudor seems to hold the
garner to which the harvestings of Border slave-nur-
series are brought before their distribution among the
plantations.   " You ask," he says to Kephart,—" you

ask about little boys and girls." (Kind-hearted Kephart! how childhood seems to call forth his profoundest interest!) Boudor replies: " All I can say is, that they are always ready sale; but they must be *purchased right*, or they do not pay much profit."

Nos. 3, 4, and 5 interest us in a certain girl, whose disposal seems to create a variety of sensations and speculations in the minds of Messrs. Kephart, Brashear, and Sims, all of " the profession." This girl, we learn from No. 3, is named Dulcena Dulceboso; and instead of being the dulcet being that her name would imply, she is termed " a hard case," and " a hard one." No. 4 mentions her thus: " I suppose that big price for the great Dulcena has not been obtained, and my own private opinion is, it never will be. White people won't sell in modern times; it would do in days of yore." Dulcena evidently did not prove tractable among these elegant gentlemen, for in No. 5, written some months later, we read: " I hope Harbin will put a 56-pound weight around the Dulcena Dulceboso's neck, and sink her in the Mississippi river, before she may ever get to Natchez." It is Brashear, professional of Natchez, who expresses himself thus fervently.

No. 6 furnishes the following extracts: " The woman Leaply bought of Mr. Thomas I sold to a Creole at $675 payable the 1st of April with 8 per cent interest and I hold a mortgage on her that was a good sale she was dam triflin." " I have some tight cases on hand Jimy Leaply for instance the double-head boy also I heard from Harbin on Yesterday saying he still had Dulcena Dulceboso on hand yet and I am inclined to believe will for some time. Ware talks of coming by to see you this spring he is a whole soul chap and the darndest whig you ever saw."

No. 7 is from another agent in New Orleans, and

gives us an affecting idea of what constitutes real human affliction to some minds: " The next thing is the girle Caroline Browner. this I cannot blame you for. she was a no. 1 looking Negro. she as been returned and her master claims of me a nother Negro in her place or $400. she it appears has fits no mistake about it. if the man insists I shall have to pay him the $400 for if he sues me I shall be the loser. this you see is trouble in fact." " The blacksmith is not sold yet."

No. 8 is from Mr. S. Grady, of Richmond, and informs us that " there is some activity in the market now for young Negroes, and they very scarce. I have sold so many Negroes lately that there is not now one girl in Jail but what is grown and only two boys—do send me some young Negroes.—To day Rachel Lockhart is sold for $587.50. This is the best. offer we have had since she was sick affecting her eyes so that she had to be blistered on the back of the neck—and Mr. Tait said I had better let her go. Sophia is laid up again."

In No. 9, Mr. Robert Windsor, of Alexandria, informs somebody that a boy bought by Mr. Webb in Brentsville is not delivered because the owner is not well, and that " he"—the " boy;" male Negroes of all ages being so called—" has gone to the neighbourhood of Bladensburg to see a woman and child." *What* woman and child he has gone to see before being " delivered" up, does not appear; nor by what name the woman and the child called him when they met and when they parted.

No. 10 is a gleam upon the darkness. Mr. Richard H. Carter writes from Rectortown, Fauquier County, as follows: " Mr. Kephart.—Dear Sir,—A few days since your agent, Mr. Bashears, bought in this neighbourhood, a woman by the name of Mima, and her child, from a Mr. Sherman. The husband of Mima lives with me; and such appears to be the distress of both parties on account of the separation, that I am induced to make an appeal to your humanity in their behalf." He then makes an offer to redeem the woman and child in a sum which is manifestly the best he can offer, since " he has already more Negroes than he actually wants," but which he feels is not up to the market possibility. " I am aware, sir," he continues, " that such cannot be your usual way of doing business, and that, if you do make any arrangement, it must proceed from a motive of humanity; but from what I learn concerning you, I am induced to hope my application will not be in vain."

No. 11 comes from the same neighbourhood, and one of the same name, and is in sad contrast with the last. Geo. Carter writes from Oatlands, Loudon County: " I have a mulatto female servant, twenty years old, a first-rate seamstress, capable of cutting out both men's and women's apparel, hearty, robust. She is for sale, and if you wish to buy her, *and will stipulate to send her to New Orleans or to the South, you shall have a bargain in her.* Her mistress has taken great pains in learning her to sew, and she is an excellent ladies' chambermaid." What this girl had done to make it necessary that she should go so far away can only be conjectured. The paper, handwriting, &c. indicate the writer to be a gentleman, as Southern gentlemen go. Is it possible that she was too near to some young scion of Oatlands at any spot nearer than New Orleans—one of the many who must be sold at once, even at ruinous rates, because they can be kept only at much more ruinous rates?

In No. 12, John T. West, of Elkton, Cecil Co., Maryland, makes earnest inquiries of Mr. J. Brewan after " 2 vary likely young Negro girls," and " ware that man lives that owens the fast race-horse wich," &c. &c.

No. 13, and last, is very suggestive, and reveals a phantom behind all these figures. It is Mr. Bacon Tait, of Richmond, who writes to Mr. Windsor : " Pray do me the favour to hand the enclosed letter *privately* to Mr. Armfield. *Don't take it to him at his house, but seek an opportunity to give it to him when none of his family can see you do so.*"

Thank God! the slave-dealer finds in woman influences he cannot trust. When the traffic in human hearts and souls is to be carried on, he wishes all parties to be apart from the faces of the wife and daughter.

The dates of the letters quoted range between 1837 and 1857. To-day, the great building wherein the business of Kephart and Co. was transacted is a prison filled with captured white rebels, and it is quite probable that a Negro stands as sentinel at the door.

CHAPTER V.

Misgivings—A pro-Slavery influence—Secession confessions—
Free schools.

IN reproducing these my memories of Slavery and the
South, it will, of course, be seen that I am giving each
incident in the frame of my present conviction. At
·the time they occurred, they gave me pain as they
gave it to others; but they never produced in me, until
many years later, any questioning of the social system
under which they took place. I was scarcely old enough
to reason, and I had no means of knowing that there was
any thing peculiar in the condition of the blacks, or
that the recurring sufferings of both whites and blacks
were any more to be questioned than the hot skies and
low fevers of our summer. I never heard Slavery mentioned as an institution, nor Negroes called " slaves"—
they being always spoken of as " servants."

When fifteen years of age, I was sent to Dickinson
College, Carlisle, Pennsylvania, where the students were
generally from Maryland and Virginia, there being only
enough from the Free States to keep alive the State pride
of the dominant element. On one occasion a slaveholder
from Maryland tried to seize a slave that had escaped
from him in the town, and in the *mêlée* he was killed.
One of our professors, Dr. McClintock, lately of Paris,
was accused of having assisted the slaves in the affair;
and there was a great excitement among the Southerners
in the college, in which I shared. I was graduated here
after a little over two years of study, and went back to

Virginia full of anti-Northern prejudices. I had learned,
however, that Slavery was an institution which did
not exist every where, and began to study it. I think
that my mind, as soon as I returned to Virginia, had
misgivings concerning the institution, and would have
gained the anti-Slavery view, had I not come under the
influence of a very strong person, who took the pains to
inspire me with his own opinions. With this gentleman,
though much his junior, I had an intimate acquaintance
and correspondence, because of my close relationship with
him. Gifted with extraordinary powers, he had attained
a philosophical and literary culture far beyond that of
any other Southern writer. At the time I speak of, he
was recognised as the leading editor of the South. Em-
bittered by some circumstances of his early life, he separated himself from society to a great extent ; and so
unsparing were his attacks upon the men and measures
which he did not like, that he had been involved already,
before mature manhood was reached, in six or seven
duels.   This editorial career was suspended, until lately,
by an appointment to an important diplomatic post in
Europe at the hands of President Pierce.

It became known to me, when, on my graduation, I
began to prepare for that to which all young Southerners
aspired, political life, that this cousin of mine had long
been undergoing intellectual and spiritual struggles of
which the world about him knew nothing.   His library,
which few had ever seen, was filled with the writings of
ancient and modern philosophy and speculation.   There
were the writings of Spinoza, Hegel, Kant, Goethe,
Fichte, Feuerbach, Fourier, Cousin, Rousseau, Voltaire,
Bacon, Carlyle, Hamilton, Emerson, Parker, and other
authors of the first calibre, filled with marginal notes,
indicating that the subjects discussed by them were those
on which his mind was bent day and night.   I found

that this " duelist" had known all the phases of faith
which the most religious thinkers have encountered; and
I did not wonder that one who had been living such a
life in the worldly and uncultivated city of Richmond
should have become morbid enough to be regarded as
a misanthropist. But the workings of his mind with
reference to Slavery were of more importance to me
at that time. He had evidently grappled with this
terrible subject at an early date, and was startled by
finding that he had come to the conclusion, with the
American fathers, that " all men are created free and
equal." His frank assertions of these, in that region,
very paradoxical views, led some of his friends and relatives to most earnest expostulations. But he was quite
equal to them in the vigour of his opinions, even at that
age, and not at all pained at being in a minority. Still
I fear that, as he grew older, the desire for the com-
manding intellectual position which he felt himself amply
competent to sustain, gave his mind a less independent
attitude than it had at first held toward this subject.
Hence, when the discussions concerning the unity of the
human race came on, the scientific advocates of the
diversity of races found in him an eager convert, and he
found in the new doctrines of race a justification of
Slavery. About this time the public was startled by
his first distinct theoretical utterance concerning Slavery,
in these words : " We hold that Negroes are not *men*, in
the sense in which that term is used by the Declaration
of Independence. Were the slaves men, we should be
unable to disagree with Wendell Phillips." He went
with me carefully through the subject of races, adducing
the well-known arguments of Agassiz in favour of their
diversity of origin, and the inferiority of the African ;
declared that the only opposition to this view was in its
supposed hostility to the Bible, which he showed good

orthodox authority for setting aside on such subjects; and, in fine, convinced me that this was the true view to take of Slavery. I seized the view with enthusiasm; it seemed to take a phantom from my path, and to liberate me for the political career to which I aspired. At the same time my relative engaged me to write for his journal, which to one of my years was flattering, and brought me into personal acquaintance with some leading public men. These were, nearly all of them, *Secessionists*, as was the relative of whom I have written at such length. Their idea, as laid before me at that time, was that the generation by which the Constitution was framed shared the universal democratic idea that all men had a right to be free and equal; that this was true with the exception of blacks, who were of an inferior race; but that the Constitution, having been framed by those who had not this more advanced view, must continually pinch upon Slavery and its normal development in the Government. Freed from the North, South America, Cuba, the Indies, Mexico, would all naturally cast themselves into our arms, and the most magnificent empire of the world would be formed.

My father was deeply pained at the influences under which I had fallen. He was a very conservative man, entirely opposed to secession, and did not hesitate to express to me his grief that I was disposed to give myself so utterly to a " doomed institution." (He was the only *man* in the South whom I have ever heard speak against Slavery; and, alas! it has been many years since I have heard of any such utterance from him.)

I was then put to be the deputy-clerk in the court of Fauquier County, Virginia, and at the same time to study at law. This court-house is at Warrenton. Whether this town was worse than any other that I had lived in, or whether the treatment of Negroes in my father's

household had been better than that class received elsewhere, or whether my eyes had grown more observant,
I cannot say; but it is certain that the licentiousness,
cruelty, and suffering appertaining to Slavery at that
town were so shameless and fearful, that they turned the
stomach. I had, indeed, come to regard Negroes as less
than men, but was not prepared to see them treated as
brutes; nay, if they were brutes, all the more bestial
were the whites, who held their female sex only for the
basest purposes. But I was admonished that these evils
were simply what grew out of every society; that, so far
as Slavery was concerned, the new scientific view must
be advanced until it was embodied into a new code of laws
which would be better; that, meanwhile, our proper
work was to seek to reform and elevate the whites, and
give them larger ideas on this and other subjects. This
view seemed to me the true one. I did not cease to feel
the wrongs of the slaves, nor to forget the special cruelties which I have elsewhere related; but I think I must
have felt them less keenly, as I turned to give my entire
attention to a project in another direction, which, however, I believed, if carried out, would cut the tap-root of
all the evils of society.

This project was the establishment of Free Schools in
Virginia.

For nearly a year I was entirely absorbed in this
idea, and devoted every spare moment that I had to
reading on the subject of school-systems. I had collected the fearful statistics of the ignorance of the people
in Virginia, and the immense losses which were trace-
able to ignorance, in the way of uncleared and un-
drained lands and unmined metals, and was preparing
to lay these surprising facts before the State Convention
which was about to meet to revise the code of laws of
the State. In the course of my studies I met with cer-

tain views on the subject of land, and the importance of
the masses having some relation to it, which interested
me in the Homestead question, or the granting of free
homes to settlers in the West, which was then the dream
of a few, and had one champion in Congress (Mr. Dodge,
of Iowa), but which has, under the present Administration, become a reality.

It was at this time (1850) that a great dinner was
given in Warrenton to Messrs. J. M. Mason and R. M.
T. Hunter, senators of the United States for Virginia.
It was immediately after the passage by Congress of what
was known as the Omnibus Bill—a compromise measure
in which the North gained the admission of California as
a Free State, and the South the infamous Fugitive Slave
Bill, the honour of framing and engrossing which belonged to Mason.   The dinner was given to these senators as an appreciation of their services in this particular.
They came and brought with them Elwood Fisher, a
renegade Quaker, who had espoused the cause of Slavery
per se, and had written a pamphlet which had been
widely circulated in the South, the object of which was
to show that the South was kept poor by its union with
the North, and that it could only begin a career of prosperity when it had separated from the North.   After
the dinner, Mr. Fisher opened the discussions with a
speech recapitulating the views of his pamphlet; and
Mason and Hunter followed with speeches in which they
declared that the admission of California as a Free State
was a grievous wrong to the South, and in itself a sufficient cause for secession; but that it was doubtful if at
that time it would be prudent to attempt secession, as the
people of the Southern States were not prepared for it.
But they advised that clubs should be formed every
where in the South to prepare the people for division,
pledging themselves that they, and other Southern repre-

sentatives at Washington, would never cease working for that end at the Capitol.

After the dinner they (the senators) came down to take tea with Colonel W. F. Phillips, the gentleman with whom I resided, and whose deputy-clerk I was. Here I had an opportunity to converse with them. On asking them something about the Homestead Law, which Mr. Dodge was trying to get through Congress, I was troubled to hear them sneer at it as an agrarian project, apiece with Abolitionism, and one which would never be passed by Congress. I ventured afterwards to lay before them my darling project for educating the people of Virginia, and was shocked to find that they regarded free schools with horror. Mason was particularly vehement in denouncing the education of the white masses, and declared that such education would be surely followed by the introduction into the South of the entire swarm of Northern "isms." Indeed, both senators treated me with coldness after they found that I was interested in giving lands to the landless and instruction to the ignorant.

Nevertheless I did not abate my efforts in the matter of free schools; but having completed my investigations and my argument, I had them published in a pamphlet, entitled, *Free Schools in Virginia*, which was distributed among the people, and laid on the desk of every member of the newly-appointed Convention for revising the State Code. But I cannot express the grief I felt at the reception which my pamphlet met at the hands of the leading men and journals of the State. It was virulently attacked as an effort to introduce into the South the worst phase of New-England society—as the effort to make a "mob-road to learning." The poor whites, it was plainly declared, must be kept ignorant; for if they were educated, they would revolutionise Southern society.

D

After this I felt that the wretchedness and ignorance of the poor whites around me, of whom I shall speak hereafter, were deliberately fostered by the higher classes. The matter assumed the nature of a battle between classes; and I was disposed to take the side of the poor, and show them how deeply wronged they were. How to reach these masses I did not know, but finally concluded to become a Methodist preacher, that Church being the one which seemed to have the most power over the middle and lower classes of Virginia. Consequently I began my studies for that ministry, and formally gave up pursuing my law studies any further.

But I must not neglect to state, that when Mason and Hunter left Warrenton, there was formed, at their suggestion, a Southern Rights Club, of which I was the secretary. This club, which was not public, met intermittently during my subsequent residence in Warrenton, and discussed the question of secession. All who belonged to it were advocates of secession, and the only difference was as to the time and method of accomplishing our great end. I remember well that the recognised difficulty at this time was, that there was still an attachment to the Union in the South, too widespread to make action at that time prudent; and also that a unanimous opinion prevailed that there would be no forcible opposition on the part of the North to such secession, chiefly because the North was made up of cowards.

CHAPTER VI.

Methodism—An oasis—A Quaker patriarch—Conversion.

I AM satisfied that every young Southerner has, at some period of his life, similar misgivings to those which beset me on my return from college as to the state of society by which he is surrounded; and that the reason why such misgivings are generally unproductive is, as in my own case, that there is within reach no other better social state with which to compare his own. Students from the South there are in some Northern colleges, it is true; but they are there when State-pride and sectional prejudice are in full sway, and the thinking and observing faculties undeveloped; and moreover the confession must be made, that the colleges of the North favoured by the South were careful to exclude such persons or books as would offend Southern prejudices. The leading Northern Universities were the last to yield to the anti-Slavery sentiment of the people. In later years the Southerners may travel through the North and through Europe; but their faculties are now as perverted as they were formerly immature; they are thoroughly committed, body and soul, to Slavery; it is Slavery that enables them to travel: to turn against that institution, then, whatever they might think of it in their hearts, would be to become penniless on the moment, and to be exiles from the circle of relationship and interest at home. Thus it is a rare thing that a Southerner, at the right age, gets a real glimpse of any society which might reveal for him the deformities of that which he has inherited.

Up to the time (1850) when I joined the Baltimore
Methodist Conference, which had supervision of all
Northern Virginia as well as Maryland, I had never
(really) seen any free society, and was unaware of the
existence of any region without the evils to which I had
become accustomed. My first appointment under the
Conference was to Rockville Circuit, which stretches from
the District of Columbia up through twenty-five miles on
the Maryland side of the Potomac. I had some twelve
different congregations in charge, comprising persons
in all conditions of society. The land and society were
generally about the same with that which I had always
known in Virginia ; but there was one section, called
Sandy Spring, which was quite different from any I had
ever seen. It was a Quaker settlement ; not, however,
a village, but a succession of finely-cultivated farms, with
pleasant residences, covering an area of eight or nine
square miles. So beautiful and cheerful was this Quaker
neighbourhood, with its bright homes and fields filled
with happy labourers,—the only happy Negroes I had
ever seen, — that I always experienced an exhilaration
in riding there, and have often gone several miles out
of my way to go through it to my appointments. I
could tell the very line on the ground where the ordinary
Maryland ended and the Quaker region began, and felt,
when I touched that line, as a wayfarer might feel on
leaving hot sands for a pleasant grove with singing-birds
and fountains.

Gradually I became interested in the Quakers, none
of whom lived in any portion of the country where I had
resided. Their plain meeting-house, situated in a beautiful grove, attracted me ; and I now and then attended
the meeting. The company generally sat in silence,
though occasionally a patriarchal old man arose and
uttered a few sentences of the Scriptures. On a certain

day, when I had been in one of these silent sittings, and was riding off, I was hailed by this old patriarch, and waited for him. "I have seen thee at our meetings several times, friend." "Yes; and I have enjoyed them." "Will thee go by my house to-day and have some dinner? I should like to speak with thee." The old man's invitation was too genuine, as was also my interest in the Friends, for me to decline; and so I paced my horse along after his carriage, until we reached his quiet home. It was a bright summer's day, and we were sitting in the porch, when he began conversation by saying that he supposed that I was interested in the Friends by my coming to their meetings, which were generally silent and unattractive to young persons. I said that he had judged truly. "And may I ask thee what has interested thee?" "Chiefly the great difference between these Quaker farms and homes, and any thing I have ever before seen." "I should like to have thee see more than the outside of our neighbourhood. We have some schools, and a library." Accordingly a day was appointed when I should return and visit a seminary in the neighbourhood, and some other places of interest. When I found, on that visit, that I was in a place where mental culture was general, —where there was a good circulating library and excellent schools,—I was as one in a dream. Again I visited the old Quaker patriarch and preacher, and told him with what delight I had found that the interior life of Sandy Spring was even more attractive than its exterior. "Now, friend, can thee account for this evident superiority of the Friends' neighbourhood over the rest of this county, or of thy own State? We are people of the same stock with those thee hast always known; the names of our families are old Maryland and Virginian names,—and yet thee sees a difference in our condition."

" Perhaps," I replied vaguely, " this is a better tract of
land than others." " That is not the case; I can remember when there were many much better sections all
around us." " Well," I again ventured, " doubtless you
Friends have certain habits of thrift and industry which
others have not." " Perhaps it is so," said the old man
gravely; after which followed a long silence, which I
felt belonged to him, and was for him to break.   Then
he turned his eyes—at once luminous and keen—full
upon me, and said: " But there is *one* habit of our
people to which thee will find, should thee search into it,
is to be traced all the improved condition of our lands
and of our homes; that is *the habit of taking care that our
labourers get just wages for their work. No slave has
touched any sod in any field of Sandy Spring.*"

These were the first words I had ever heard uttered
against Slavery in itself.   They were spoken to one who
still held to the doctrine that the Negro was not the
brother of the Caucasian, and who was but a few weeks
ago the secretary of a Secession Club.   The old man had
spoken as he was moved, and there was a certain glory
on his white hairs as he did so; but, like those shep-
herds watching in the night, when this new star rose for
me I was sore afraid.   Here I was sitting under the
roof, and as it were at the feet, of one of those Abolitionists from whom I and my comrades were to sever
our beloved South for ever !   I was not exactly offended
at what the Quaker said, but was exceedingly disquieted,
and, having let the subject drop, soon departed.

I did not see my old friend for many months afterwards, but the seed which he had dropped into my mind
had a vitality beyond all others that had been implanted.
I confess that I struggled against it; for already I was
committed to interests and relations in life which would
be utterly revolutionised and overthrown by any confes-

sion of anti-Slavery opinions. But though pain and despair grew with it, the seed grew; in vain did I cease visiting Sandy Spring, where every garden and happy labour reminded me of that Quaker habit of giving the labourer his wages; the rest of the land, with its waste places and its paupers and huts, groaned out their testimony to the old man's words.

Then all society and life seemed to change about me. Had all the slaveholders of Maryland been suddenly seized with an epidemic that they should begin to maltreat their slaves? Was it a conspiracy that I could scarcely visit one of the families of my circuit, but I should witness scenes of cruel parting between the helpless people, whose pangs were often too lucrative to be spared? Was the overseer with his lash a new institution? Or were these things but the revelations to an awakened sense of what has been going on for generations around millions who never saw them, and would at this moment deny that they ever occurred? I searched backward into my past life, and was startled to find that there arose memories, hitherto dumb and sleeping,—memories of greater wrongs than those I now saw,—which joined with these to force upon me the clear perception that there was a great Wrong coiled about the land, and that it was SLAVERY.

Nevertheless the idea of coping with the evil thus revealed, personally, was very slow in entering my mind. So accustomed had I been to regard Slavery as the very corner-stone of society; so bound hand and foot by my relations to it; so awed by that illusion of power with which a great Social Wrong can invest itself,—that my new perception seemed to me to be a terrible secret, to be hushed and held down in my own breast. About this time, however, I was deeply moved by something that occurred within what had been my own charge. There was at Sandy Spring a family connected with the Methodist Church, consisting of a father and three daughters; the mother had been dead many years. The gentleman owned a good farm, and a considerable number of slaves. The family was very pleasant, but each of its members was in delicate health. Not long after my appointment to another circuit in an adjacent county, I heard that the father and one of his daughters had died. Passing through that neighbourhood a few months later, I called with the expectation of seeing the remaining daughters. But I found that on the death of their father these girls, whom he had left in comfortable circumstances, had at once liberated all their slaves, and, having sold the farm in order to give the poor creatures a start in the world, went themselves—delicate as they were—to earn their own livelihood in Philadelphia with (I believe) their needles.

I have never seen them since; but I think it was when I turned away from that door with this narrative in my heart that I resolved to enlist openly against Slavery.

At this time I was the junior minister on Frederick Circuit, and resided for most of the time in Middletown Valley, Maryland, which is inhabited chiefly by Germans, who do their own work, and own few or no slaves. I had but little opportunity here for becoming acquainted with slaves; but my impression was, that they were generally unconscious of the degradation of their condition, and had little desire for freedom. Before the year was out, however, some changes in my religious views, added to my new anti-Slavery convictions, led me to resign my ministerial charge; and at my father's request I went back to his house in Virginia. I had thus far told only him and my mother of my new views concerning Slavery; and whilst my father was stricken with grief at my evident determination to avow and advocate the abolition of Slavery, my mother indicated less anxiety concerning the fate of the institution than that of myself. They had both resolved, however, to keep my new views secret even from the rest of the family; and my father hoped to persuade me from being an Abolitionist. I accepted his invitation to visit Falmouth; the understanding being that I should not converse with any slave on the subject of his condition, or tamper with the Negroes in any way.

I have already said that I had not seen any thing to induce me to believe that the slaves desired freedom; indeed, with the few anti-Slavery men whom I had met, I had stoutly maintained, against their views, this indifference to freedom as the most degrading and the strongest fetter which bound the slave. But now, when I came home, I found that in some way the Negroes knew what my parents believed to be a secret between them and myself. It is barely possible that my new views showed themselves unconsciously in my manner; but, however that may be, I found the Negroes at Falmouth, including some of my father's, anxious to have secret interviews with me as to their condition. Of course, I kept my promise to my father; but I expressed my astonishment to them, that in all the years that I had known them, I had before seen no sign of this yearning for freedom; to which they replied, that it was because in all those years they had seen no sign of the Abolitionist about me. From that moment I felt that the social system of the South was undermined. If such feelings were lurking in the breasts of Negroes in one of the obscurest portions of Virginia, where a Northern man had never been seen,—and among those, too, who were the most kindly treated,—to such an extent as to enable them to divine the slightest and most carefully-concealed disposition in their favour, I knew that there must be a far wider discontent among them in other regions.

Many years ago an artist of Philadelphia was engaged by the State of South Carolina to paint some national emblematic picture for her State-house. Jefferson Davis was requested to act with the South-Carolina Committee at Washington in criticising the studies for this work. The most creditable sketch presented was a design representing the North by various mechanical implements; the West by a prairie and plough; whilst the South was represented by various things, the centre-piece, however, being a cotton-bale with a Negro upon it fast asleep. When Mr. Davis saw it, he said, " Gentlemen, this will never do: what will become of the South when that Negro wakes up?"

The Southerners have certainly counted upon the continued sleep of the Negro; but it has only needed the glimpse of the Union banner marked EMANCIPATION to reveal to their astonishment that the Negro has been long awake, notwithstanding his closed eyelids.

CHAPTER VII.

Northward—The fugitive Burns—Exile.

AFTER the change in my religious views, which led me to resign my place in the Methodist Church, I went to the North, and entered the Divinity College at Cambridge, Massachusetts. It was not long afterwards that the great excitement at the arrest of Anthony Burns, a fugitive slave, occurred at Boston. Anthony was born in the village of Falmouth; and I had personally known him and his master, C. F. Suttle, all my life. At this time he, then about twenty years of age, had made his way, through many hardships and dangers, to Massachusetts and Freedom—as he hoped. His master and another, whom I knew well, came on to Boston, and Burns was discovered and arrested. Boston soon swarmed with an angry multitude; and President Pierce, always the willing tool of Slavery, took care to have several regiments of soldiers there to suppress any attempt at rescue. Chains were stretched around the United States Court-House, which was closely guarded also, under which the judges and lawyers had to bend on entering: such chains, alas, at that time, clanked wherever the American flag waved.

There were at this time many Southern students at Cambridge; and as there was every probability that there would be an attempt on the part of the enraged people to prevent the rendition of Burns, these young Southerners got together, and concluded to offer their sympathy to the slave-hunters from Virginia, and their assistance if it were required. They called upon me to go with them. I told them that I sympathised entirely with the fugitive, and if I entered into the affair at all, it would be on his side. Of course this was at once told to Mr. Suttle. When the United States President and his army at last won their glorious victory over poor Tony, and he was taken back to Virginia, his master did not fail to let it be known that the only fellow-townsman he had in Boston—myself—had been opposed to him. To this day that slaveholder does not know that if I had consented to be the spy which some desired me to be, and, by calling on him simply as a fellow-townsman, learned and reported his quarters to the crowd, he never would have lived to take his slave home or to denounce me.

I need not attempt to repeat the execrations which returned to me from Virginia when it was reported that I had become an Abolitionist, or the expressions of terror and grief from my relations, many of whom declared that they had rather have heard of my death. There was, however, a sweet compensation in the fact that I then first discovered, that my mother had in her heart cherished for many years a fervent hatred of Slavery. Every Southern woman has, God knows, enough reason to hate it; and my conviction is, that many of those very women at the South who are so violent against the Northern soldiers, are yet secretly praying that in the storm of battle that monster which feeds upon the purity of sons and husbands may be pierced by some fatal arrow.

Yet I indulged the dream that I might return to my native State still most dearly loved, and plead with those whom I knew against Slavery. And so soon as I was graduated at Cambridge (1854), I returned, with all hope and eagerness, to my home in Virginia. Alas, it was to find that thenceforth I had no home there for ever; it was to be chilled by the sneers and coldness of those who once loved me; to find that my most intimate friends of former days would not appear with me in the street; and that many of those whose blood I shared regarded me as a leper. As soon as it was known in the town that I had arrived, I was confronted in the street by a company of young men, most of them my former schoolmates and friends, who told me that I was spared tar and feathers only for the sake of my father and other relatives, and on the condition that I should leave the State for ever. Thus, without ever having uttered a word of interference with master or slave, I was exiled from the spot where I was born, simply for an honest conviction that Freedom was better than Slavery.

At length, then, I left Virginia, — penniless, and almost friendless, — and with a heavy foreboding that the society which thus cast out those who loved them, and would try to free them gently and kindly from the blighting curse, must in the end pass away with the wrong it hugs.

I have often thought that, next to the accusation against Slavery to be fouud in the cries of the crushed slaves themselves, the bitterest is to be found in the anguish of those who have seen it freezing all the pulses of natural affection which had been wont to flow toward them. That institution seems actually to have been so worshipped as at length to have been invested with the awful power of creating a generation of human beings in its own image and likeness; one which, at its faintest wish, is willing to sacrifice to its idol all that is human or generous. For that no heart is too dear to be repulsed; for it the fairest and longest growths of relationship and friendship will be instantly torn up by the roots. Not one Southerner who has ever uttered a word against Slavery has ever been suffered to remain in the South. Again and again have I met these exiles,—the Helpers, Underwoods, Goodloes; and sometimes tender women, as the Grimkes and Mattie Griffiths,—who had once fond homes and bright hopes in the South; but at the touch of one thought not servile to Slavery, all these crumbled in an instant, and they were forced to wander to ungenial climates and strange lands, to begin life anew, if heart and strength for that remained.

But so long as Slavery ruled in America, there was no region where this remorseless spirit was not felt. The rich and powerful every where united in the worship of that which had wrapped itself in the flag of the country, and held its most important purse-string; and though the anti-Slavery man was no longer cast into a dungeon as was Garrison, or murdered as was Lovejoy, there was a bleak Siberia in the heart of every community to which he was sent. They who wandered to the North found Wendell Phillips banished from the society in which he was born, and of which he would otherwise have been the darling, living apart from his former companions, and unvisited by many of his nearest relatives. When, called to a church in Washington City, I went there to reside, even so late as 1854, I found Charles Sumner, and the few anti-Slavery men then in Congress, utterly ignored by Washington society, and cohering into a little Massachusetts of their own.

No sooner had I begun to call the attention of my congregation—the most liberal in Washington—to the wrongs of the Negro, than one after another I found my warmest friends abandoning me and my church; and when, at last, I went from the bedside of Sumner—brought to the verge of death by the tomahawk of Slavery—to denounce the barbarity of the system which would stop at no outrage, the congregation were paralysed with terror, the choir refused to sing the closing hymn, and I was permitted to meet my congregation but once more, after urgent solicitation, and that only to bid them farewell.

Yet I felt and saw that this exasperation of Slavery was a confession of its mistrust; that which feels itself strong does not need so many bolts and bars. The body-guard of Slavery had not, then, the calmness of real strength, nor the serenity of those who feel that the future is for them.

CHAPTER VIII.

Slavery logical—The practical working of slave-codes—Their
downward development.

It is claimed by some, that the slave-laws, which only
need to be quoted to shock the moral sense of every
civilised man, are merely the relics of barbarous times,
which linger only in form, and are practically inopera-
tive.   This is not the case.   The earlier codes of the
Southern States were much more merciful to the Negroes
than those which now exist.   In most of the Southern
States the codes have been revised within the last fifteen
or twenty years; and whilst, with regard to Slavery,
none of their provisions have been mitigated, in many
States they have been rendered more severe.   This was
the case in Virginia, where the code was revised in 1849.
The worst of the slave-laws are those which punish in-
ordinately any resistance whatever by a Negro to a
white man, no matter what cruelty or wrong may be
done to himself or his family; which prohibits the reception of a Negro's testimony in court against a white
man, whether the Negro be free or a slave; and which
forbids all mental instruction of Negroes.   Nevertheless
I have lived long enough in contact with Slavery to
know that not one of these laws is illogical or unnecessary to the system.   Once grant to Slavery the right
of existence, and those laws must be recognised as the
essential conditions of that right.   Discipline on the
plantations would be at an end if the slave could legally
resist, or could assault his master and receive as punishment only the stripes to which he is accustomed.   If the

Negro's testimony were received in court against his master, it would be an over-strong temptation for him to wield that powerful weapon against his oppressor, even by false charges; whilst even with true ones, two-thirds of the overseers and masters could not remain out of prison a month. Slavery was born of a patriarchal autocracy, and in whatsoever age or land it survives, it must preserve about it the same absolute impunity. The education of Negroes has been again and again tried, for the Southerners know as well as others that educated labourers are the most valuable; but it was shown, by indisputable evidence, that every Negro was discontented with the condition of a slave in the proportion of his education. The external fetter of the slave depends for its chief strength upon the internal one which binds him to brutehood. Slavery is thus forced to obey its own dark laws, and is pitiless, not because Southern human nature rejoices in the infliction of pain, but because Slavery is not a free agent. They can move only on the terrible grooves to which they have committed themselves. Evil is as organic as good; the cancer has as systematic a development as the eye; Slavery is chained as much as the slave.

Those in the South who could not shut their eyes to the monstrous crime of closing up every avenue to knowledge or humanisation against a whole race, have generally been forced to the conclusion that the Slave States have followed the system to its logical results, and have deliberately determined to abide by them. Mr. Samuel M. Janney, of Loudon Co., Virginia, a distinguished Quaker minister, who had already been arrested and fined for speaking, "as the spirit moved him," against the wrongs around him, united with me, soon after my exile from Virginia, in framing a petition to the Legislature of our State (for I never consented to give up my citizenship in Virginia),

E

entreating them to repeal the law which forbade the teaching of slaves to read,—simply that,—and to enact such laws as would prevent the arbitrary separation of husband and wife, parent and child. A few signatures were obtained to this petition, and it was sent; but it was never read in the Legislature of Virginia. Yet a private reply came from a leading member of the Legislature, declaring that no such petition could be read in that body; that the evils we deplored were essential to the system of Slavery; that education, it had been proved, rendered slaves discontented; that it was a virtual denial of a man's property in his slaves if he were not permitted to sell them, whatever their relationship, as his interests or obligations demanded; that all social systems must have some evils, and that those of the South were no greater than the evils of other countries. About the same time a petition of the same kind was drawn up by Mr. Goodloe, a North-Carolinian, now a resident of Washington, and sent to the Legislature of his native State. This was numerously signed, but it was never read in the Legislature that I have heard. Hence nothing has been left to the Southerners whose eyes were opened to the iniquity but to protest against it; and for this they have invariably been killed or driven to the North. Thus the South has been for years separating from itself every influence which would have mitigated the evils of Slavery, and, having retained those only who were abject worshippers of their cruel idol, have swiftly gone from depth to depth in fulfilment of its remorseless necessities.

This obvious downward development of Slavery into severer laws and usages is admitted in the South, and charged upon the Abolitionists, who, it is said, by their agitations and the institution of methods for the escape of slaves, have made stricter laws and harder fetters necessary. " You," cries the South bitterly, — " you Abolitionists have been the foes of the slave ; you have made his lot harder ; even in South America the slave-laws are milder because there is no Abolition-party seeking to destroy their institution." If this plea, which is the reverse side of a truth, be analysed, it amounts only to an admission that American Slavery is such an anachronism, and so counter to the spirit of the New World, that its existence must be defended, if at all, by the coarse and violent measures and methods of barbarous ages. The Czar defends his proceedings toward Poland, and Austria its stern measures in Venetia, by the same simple logic : their victims have only to lie still in their hands, and the rigours will cease. Nor have they failed to accuse the freer peoples of Western Europe of helping to keep alive the insubordinate spirit in their subjects, and thus rendering stronger chains necessary. Whilst we deplore the immediate evils, the increased sorrows, which may come of the attempt to eradicate a wrong, we see in them the working of a law which must be submitted to. The pangs of amputation are sharper than those of mortification, yet one in the end saves and the other kills the patient. The tightening of the chains that bind men is painful indeed, but when they are most galling they are nearest to breaking. The anti-Slavery men of America have simply been true to the light of this age, and have opened the eyes of a nation to see the fearful wrong it was fostering : that was their duty, whatever the temporary result to the slave ; for his fetters they were not responsible, for their duty they were. Their faith has been justified by the event ; for although the slave may for the moment have suffered more, the system which made him a slave was compelled to show, one after another, its hitherto unsuspected possibilities of crime ; to show that, for its power to own and trade in human beings, it was willing to reduce them to actual brutality—to hold them by any cruelty—to quench the very flame of God in them. The reformer is never wiser than when he forces evil to " fill up the measure of its iniquities :" Slavery, compelled by the roused conscience of the North to fulfil its own nature, is now doing so, and thereby committing suicide.

Almost all the cruelties of Slavery are to be regarded as the work of the law, which is an accomplice of every wrong which it does not try to prevent. But besides the immediate suffering endured by slaves from the arbitrary rule of their masters, the sad extent to which the very heart and manhood of the race is eaten into by this utter denial of all the usual protections and institutions which denote humanity, can scarcely be estimated. It was, I think, about the year 1847 that our county was much agitated by an approaching election for a State delegate. One of the candidates was a Mr. B., who was a very bad man indeed. Walking into the field on the morning of the election, I found an aged Negro quietly at work, with whom I was fond of conversing. The old man gave me a greeting, and I asked him who, in his opinion, would be elected that day. The old slave leaned on his hoe-handle, and said, " Cap'n B., I specs." " But, uncle, you wouldn't like to have him elected ?" " Don' know 's I would ; but it don' matter what we niggers 'd like, mars'r." " Captain B.'s servants don't like him much, uncle, do they ?" " You ask mars'r what *he* knows 'bout Cap'n B. Bless ye, chile ! ye wasn't more 'n dis high when a man rode up hard 's he could ride to the door, 'n told mars'r dat Cap'n B. had kilt his big Jim. He cum to mars'r 'case, ye see, mars'r was a jestice. ' How 'd he kill him ?' says mars'r. Says the man, ' Our Dolly, as works with Cap'n B., told our niggers, wen she came home last night, that Cap'n B.

had been a-beatin' big Jim all day, and she lef him
a-beatin' ov him, an' he swore that he wouldn' leave
bref in him.   An' dis mornin' the cap'n he rid over an'
ordered a coffin from Snellings fur his man Jim.'   'Who
saw dis beatin' a-goin' on?' says mars'r, turnin' pale.
' Only de niggers,' says de man.   Den mars'r he jump
up, and clench his fists, an' say, ' Den 'tain't no more 'n
ef de cows 'n pigs see him do it.   It's no use a-goin'
to the cor'ner.   De man must be buried as de cap'n
wishes, an' den he may go on an' kill all his niggers fur
what I kin help.'   Den de man went away, an' mars'r
went into his office, 'n lock de door.   'Twas afore breakfas' an' afore prars, 'n mars'r sent up word dat dere
wouldn' be no prars dat mornin', and dat he didn' wan'
no breakfas'.   But ebery body know Cap'n B. kill big
Jim ; but only niggers seen it, and nigger nobody.
Cap'n be 'lected, I specs.   Knows all 'bout de laws, I
spec.   Knows *wen* he may kill a nigger, an' wen he
mayn't.   Bless ye, chile ! niggers seein' a thing ain't
more 'n so many pine-trees."

A missionary from America, who has spent twenty
years at Gaboon in Africa, told me, that although the
Africans in their native land were not so tamed as the
Negroes he had seen in our Southern States, there was
about them a *flavour* of character, a distinctiveness of race,
which he had vainly looked for in the Negroes of America.   I fancy that this is so ; and that this tameness,
which the Southerners call their Christianisation, is
simply the destruction of the tissues of manhood in them
by their legal non-existence as human beings.   Rude
as their laws in Africa are, they are an expression of
their race, and all have a vital relation to them ; though
wild men, they are men ; but in the Slave States their
spirit as a race is broken, their hope of a future on earth
quenched, and the feeling of race in atrophy.   Were

wildness and confusion to be the immediate result of setting them free, the philanthropist might find in that
condition a step upward.

As indicating the extent to which the slave-codes
ignore the humanity of Negroes, I may quote a case
quite recently decided in the courts of Virginia, with
the facts of which I have a personal acquaintance.   Adjoining my father's estate, on the Stafford side of the
Rappahannock, was a fine mansion and estate, known as
Chatham.   It had belonged to a distinguished judge (Coalter), and at his death fell into the hands of his widow.
There were nearly one hundred slaves connected with
the estate, who had always been treated kindly.   Mrs.
Coalter lived with her daughters entirely alone on this
estate, her mansion being a mile from any other ; she
employed no white overseer, and had no white resident
on the estate, the management of which was intrusted
absolutely to one of her slaves.   Under this man the
lands yielded finely, and the family wealth continued.
Mrs. Coalter further secured the devotion of her slaves
by assuring them frequently that at her death they
should all be free.   Many of her acquaintances—I myself
among the number—had heard her declare that she had
so provided for these Negroes.   But one of her relatives,
a lawyer, who was called in to give the will a legal
form, persuaded her to alter the clause giving the slaves
their freedom, and make it read that they should have
their freedom if they should so choose, and if not, that
they should select for themselves owners from among
her blood-relatives.   The old lady, in her simplicity,
had her will so written, and soon after died.   No sooner
had this occurred, than one Lacy, who had become by
marriage her next heir, entered court with a claim, that
*since the laws recognised slaves only as chattels, they did
not and could not be allowed to have the power of legal*

choice as to their condition. The inferior courts decided in favour of Lacy. It was carried through the Supreme Court of Virginia, which confirmed the decision of the lower courts, one judge (Moncure), however, having denounced it as a flagrant oppression of the defenceless, in such terms as to bring tears to the eyes of many in the court-room. But the code had no more power of choice than the slaves; and so the State of Virginia deliberately joined with Lacy in robbing ninety-five human beings of their liberty.

But there was a higher than the Supreme Court of that State, a Court where the appeals of the wronged are always heard. It was only four or five years after the above decision by the Supreme Court of Virginia, that Major-General McDowell, of the United States, had his head-quarters at Chatham, and Lacy, now a Confederate officer, was a prisoner at Washington, and all of his slaves free. Even the heathen knew that "Justice, being overturned, will overturn."

CHAPTER IX.

The Negro—The new (scientific) way to pay old debts—Wages
—European blood enslaved in the Southern States—Dr.
Hunt on the Negro's place in Nature—Points of inferiority
and of superiority—The moral, mental, and physical characteristics of the American Negro—Miscegenation.

MONTESQUIEU said that it would not do to agree that
Negroes are men, lest it should then appear that the
whites are not.

In 1781, in the case of the ship *Zong,* whose master
had thrown 132 slaves alive into the sea to cheat the
underwriters, the first jury gave a verdict in favour of
the master and owners : they had a right to do what
they had done.   Lord Mansfield is reported to have said
on the bench : " The matter left to the jury is, Was it
from necessity ?   For they had no doubt — though it
shocks one very much—that the case of slaves was the
same as if horses had been thrown overboard."   From
this depth it was that the heart of the British nation
recoiled, until it gave to her history one of those days
which men celebrate throughout the civilised world as
affording the real evidence of man's superiority to inferior orders.

And yet—for there is such a thing as *recurrence* in
mind as well as in physics—we have to-day those who are
seeking to get from the great Tribunal of Nature a re-
versal of this later decree, which declared that the case of
the slaves and that of the horses were eternally different ;
and a return to the old law, by general consent, at the
very moment when the Heavens are raining fire upon

the only nation that dared to try and retain it after the crime had been unveiled!

The first thing that strikes one in the scientific Evangel of Slavery is the greeting it must receive from those philosophers—not few in this world—who have always felt a profound, but hitherto unexplained, aversion toward paying those little bills with which, in the present disordered condition of the world, any inferior may annoy a person of condition. You have only to employ a washerwoman who stoops, a shoeblack with a hare-lip, and to take care that your cabman has a retreating chin or wide nose; and then, if change is demanded, you have simply to decline firmly and anthropologically. True, the law may be against you; but was it not also against Socrates? Only plant yourself firmly on the principle that a flat foot, a long heel, or a diminished facial angle, cancels all such obligation, and the world may come round to you, and our courts learn to settle cases between debtor and creditor by measuring *pelves* and *pollices!*

If there be such a law in this universe as justice, one must decide that it, for the first time, reveals itself, or has any need to reveal itself, as a law where *un*equals are concerned, and that by it

" No god dare wrong a worm."

Antecedent to all questions of high or low " place in Nature" of any human or other creature, is the principle of fair pay for work done. The word *wage* is another form of *gauge;* wages are the honest measure or balance to a worker for work done. The horse and ox must have their wages; must be cared for with reference to the amount or kind of work they are required to do. Now, here is a worker, say, who, though inferior to his employer, is required to do, and does, such work as requires

thought and feeling as well as physical toil.   He has, let
us suppose, demanded wages.

Employer. I give you what I give other animals—
food and shelter.

Workman. But I do different work from theirs.
Some thought went with my sinews; also there was
some human feeling of what a man or his home might
need, which enabled me to serve your higher wants.

E. What wages, then, do you expect?

W. Simply, that to the shelter and food of the horse
shall be added, in my case, shelter for affections and food
for mind.

E. In other words, you wish a home and education.

W. Exactly.

E. But a home means that you shall own your wife
and children, whereas *I* must own them.   And by
education I find that you are sure to become less of an
animal and more of a man.   Intellect grows by what it
feeds on; and *will* is a part of it.   I find the animal and
the man just properly balanced for my purposes.   I have
arranged your lot; go work in it.

W. Then my wages are not the honest measure of
the work I do, but the measure of your own selfishness;
so that if it were for " your own purposes" that body
should be starved as well as mind—

E. (*showing raw-hide*). To work, you scoundrel!

Thus, estimating the Negro simply as a more finely-
organised animal, Slavery is an effort to form society
after the plan of that " unjust balance" which the Maker
of this world has in many ways declared to be an abomi-
nation unto him.   Estimate him simply as an animal,
yet he is an animal that knows what it is to smile, to
weep, to love, to worship.   Are those not fine nerves?
Must there not be some exquisite brain - formation
there?   Would not a zoologist declare that, to take such

sentient brain and nerves to manure cotton-fields and sugar-cane, is anarchy and subversion—as if the British Museum were burnt to boil somebody's pot?

But, it is replied, the Negro has no affections that can be outraged ; see, here is a traveller who tells you that he consents that his wife and daughter shall be common property. He has no intellect to be improved ; here are dozens who testify that he can never learn any thing.

Ah, well ! perhaps the slaveholders will consent to alter their laws, so that, in case a Negro strikes a white man in defending wife and daughter from outrage, he shall be held excusable ? And perhaps they will consent to repeal those laws in every State which prohibit the teaching of any thing to a slave ? Of course, if a Negro has no depth in his affections, and cannot learn any thing, those laws are meaningless, and may as well be repealed. Yet is there not something significant in the *existence* of such laws ? Do they not show that the slaveholder knows better the nature of this black man whom he is holding, than those who go about seeking here and there little separate incidents and cases to justify their foregone conclusions ?

But, it is again replied, these superiorities of mind and feeling are found with the American Negroes because so many of them have their blood mixed with that of the white race. Very well ; then so far as Slavery in America is concerned, the scientific question of the Negro's position can be of very little import, since the great mass of slaves have in them this mixed blood. The Abolitionist might very safely have compromised with the slaveholder on the condition of having all slaves not pure Negroes emancipated. It is indeed a rare thing in the Southern States to see a really black man ; and such a Negro passing through our streets, as I have generally observed, would attract attention and comment. Let the defenders

of the Southern Confederacy, then, meet the charge that
Slavery is systematically dwarfing Anglo-Saxon intellect
and aspiration as represented in three out of the four
millions of slaves in whom that higher blood has been
infused! Let them give their views of Slavery when it
comes in the shape of the following notice from the New
Orleans *Era :*

" WHITE MEN, BEWARE!—We are informed that a
considerable number of coloured persons, *who cannot be
distinguished from whites without close scrutiny,* have re-
gistered their names, in the hope of being able to vote
for Flanders, the champion of Negro suffrage, at the
polls to-day."

Nevertheless, in behalf of that smaller proportion of
the slaves in whom no other blood than that of the Negro
is perceptible, I utterly deny that the theory of their
unimprovability is tenable. It is, antecedently, highly
improbable that while an acre of ground, a breed of sheep,
a wild rose, a gourd, an almond, can be improved to the
verge of, if not into, a new species, a higher species than
any of them cannot be. It at least could only be maintained that such is the case after the experiment had been
tried and had failed, which is here the reverse of the fact.
There are, on the contrary, many instances of pure Negroes, and those in whom the Negro blood largely pre-
dominated, who have been eminent for their attainments.
Benjamin Banneker, of Maryland, a black Negro, whose
mother, and certainly one of his grand-parents, were
natives of Africa, had the most scientific mind which the
South has produced ; his genius as an astronomer having
been recognised by Thomas Jefferson whilst president,
and also by Condorcet. Banneker compiled the first alma-
nac and constructed the first clock ever made in America.
Charles L. Remond, whose eloquence received a high
encomium from the orator Henry Clay, a slaveholder, is

quite dark. Sojourner Truth, whose singular wit has been the subject of a paper by Mrs. Stowe ; and Harriet Tubman, better known as " Moses," on account of her having, since her escape from Slavery, returned into the very heart of the South more than twenty times and assisted hundreds of Negroes to escape,—are black. Dr. Johnson, who lately took his degree at the University of Edinburgh, and the Negro (whose name I have not learned) who has just taken a double-first degree at the University of Toronto, are jet black. So also is William Crafts, who travelled a thousand miles for freedom as the body-servant of his wife (almost white), who disguised herself as a Southern gentleman ; and who, whether as an inventor, an African explorer, or a defender of the humanity of his own race, is too well known in England to call for further notice here. These, and many others who have shown superiority and susceptibility to culture, despite the disparagements of their position, indicate sufficiently where, if ordinary fair play were allowed it, the black race might at length come to stand.

And here it may be remarked, that the professional champions of Negro inferiority exhibit at this point logical feats of the most surprising character. In Dr. James Hunt's pamphlet on *The Negro's Place in Nature* —quite valuable as a repository of all that ever was or can be said against a Negro—we learn on one page, that the mixture of the European and of the Negro results in a monster, in which whatever is " worst in the Europeans and Negroes is united," so that " they are the sink of both," and that even the continued fertility of such mixture is doubtful ; and on another page the author, lured by another point to be proved, maintains, and promises in future to show, " that nearly all the Negroes who are asserted to have arrived at any mental distinction had European blood in their veins ;" and " that, of the fifteen celebrated Negroes whose histories were collected by Abbé Gregoire, there is not one who is of pure Negro blood."

As the pamphlet just referred to is a careful summing up of all the arguments on that side, and is their latest expression, I propose to consider briefly the points made.

Dr. Hunt quotes from many sources, authentic and otherwise, the differences of the Negro from the European. It has long been known, if I mistake not, that the Negro differs in many regards from the other races. So do they from him. The questions then are, Are those differences in his favour, or otherwise ? or are some of them for, and others against him ? and in the general balancing of the account, is there such a preponderance of inferiorities as to sink him to a degree below the political and social rank assigned by theoretical consent to other races ? Now, the author of this pamphlet has so firmly settled down to the affirmative side of this last question, and argues in its favour so vehemently, that an unsuspicious reader, who has gone through his enumeration of the differences, may easily be deceived into thinking that all the facts converge to that conclusion ; and when, as I shall presently show, statements not authentic, and some even of known falsity, are carefully interpolated here and there to give their colour to the rest, the danger of error is simply proportionate to the credibility of the author. Thus, when Dr. Hunt estimates that the Negro's heel is longer than that of the European, it would, were it true, prove that in that respect the European is nearer to the ape than the Negro ; for the ape has no heel, properly speaking. Again, the writer says : " Vrolik has asserted that the pelvis of the male Negro bears a great resemblance to that of the lower mammalia." What Vrolik does say is, that " the pelvis of the male (Negro), were it taken from certain wild-beasts, could not be of a firmer substance or have a stronger bone." Now, did

Dr. Hunt mean to pervert Vrolik's meaning? or does he really think that a weak pelvis is nobler than a strong one? Elsewhere the author, in the excitement of hunting down the hated race, speaks of the hardness and whiteness of their teeth as indications of inferiority ; as if the comparatively weak teeth of the European were more to be coveted than the proverbially beautiful and finely-proportioned teeth of the African ! Coming at length to the physiological characteristics of the Negro, we are told that his senses are dull ; and, incredible as it may seem, the author quotes to prove this the following tribute of Pruner Bey to the self-control and fortitude of that race : " Bad treatment," says Pruner Bey, " causes the Negro, the Negress, and the child to abundantly shed tears ; but physical pain never provokes them. The Negro frequently resists surgical operations ; but when he once submits, he fixes his eyes on the instrument and the hand of the operator without any mark of restlessness or impatience. *The lips, however, change colour, and the sweat runs from him during the operation.* A single example will support our view : A Negress underwent the amputation of the right half of the lower jaw with the most astonishing apathy ; but no sooner was the diseased part removed, than she commenced singing with a loud and sonorous voice, in spite of our remonstrances, and the wound could only be dressed after she had finished her hymn of grace." From the same writer he quotes, as an indication of inferiority, the testimony to the Negro's peaceableness : " He has no love for war ; he is only driven to it by hunger. War from passion or destructiveness is unknown to him." What a degraded beast he must be !

Now, these and many other facts cited to prove inferiority, prove just the reverse ; and lest this should be felt by his reader, Dr. Hunt, F.R.S.* (which a shrewd

* I have lately heard this title denied Dr. H.

Yankee interprets as Foolish Rebel Sympathiser), sows an abundant quantity of tares among them in the shape of untruths asserted and insinuated. We are told that the Negro rarely stands erect. Any one who is acquainted with Negroes, or who has examined the models and skeletons of that race in the British Museum and the Royal College of Surgeons, will know that this assertion is utterly groundless. Again, his voice is declared to be thin and squeaky, resembling " the alto of an eunuch." What a misnomer then, after all, is " Negro Minstrels"! This is ridiculously false ; the Negro is remarkable for his fine voice. Amongst the hundreds of Negroes whom I have known, I do not remember one poor voice, and have rarely heard of one who could not sing finely. We have in the United States many Negro orators—Douglass, Clarke, Dulany, Brown, and others — whose superior voices are themes of remark with all that have heard them. . Those who are acquainted with the African languages agree as to their musical characteristics. I lately heard a missionary repeat, on board a steamship, before a mixed company, the Lord's Prayer as rendered into one of the Gaboon dialects ; and its remarkable melodiousness elicited a burst of applause from all who heard it. Equally untrue is it that the Negroes " have never constructed a grammatical language." In some respects, moreover, their language presents characteristics higher than the English. M. Maury remarks upon the richness of the Congo languages in the modes of the verb. Thus, the verb *sala* means, to labour ; *salila*, to facilitate labour ; *salisia*, to labour with somebody ; *salanga*, to be in the habit of labouring ; *salisionia*, to labour one for another ; *salangana*, to be skilful in labour. Concerning the dialects of the South-African families, Wilson declares that they are soft and pliable, and their grammatical principles founded on the most philosophical basis. " There are," he adds, " perhaps no languages in the world capable of more definiteness and precision of expression." Again, the tribe known as the Veys have done what it is here alleged no African race has done—invented an alphabet ; a feat, by the way, which few of the most gifted races have achieved.

In the next place, we have in this pamphlet a series of statements, partly true, partly not, which are strained to seem to prove what they do not prove. Thus, it is said that the average height of the Negro is less than that of the European. Well, the average height of the giraffe is greater than either. Brown spots on the *pia mater* are mentioned, although as common in the European as the Negro. The Negro, it is declared, is not fond of hard work; but neither was Dr. Johnson, nor Mr. Thackeray, who said : " I never take up the pen without an effort; I work only from necessity." We should scarcely regard these as inferior specimens of Humanity on that account. We do not, in America, regard Ralph Waldo Emerson as beneath the average man ; yet he wrote, with some scorn :

" 'Tis the day of the chattel—
Web to weave, and corn to grind ;
Things are in the saddle,
And ride mankind."

As for the Negroes of the West Indies, Cuba, and America, with regard to whom the charge is generally made, it may be suggested that they have already had a pretty long term of physical toil ; and that a desire for some proportionate rest, and for leisure to cultivate something besides cotton and sugar, is quite excusable in them, and perhaps approvable.

It is stated, also, and reiterated as a very important fact, that the Negroes, when taught, learn quickly up to the age of twelve or fourteen, when they become very

F

slow and dull of comprehension.   The inference is supposed to be, that there is a normal arrest of the faculties
of this race at the point where the European begins his
development.   But it has been my lot to have much to
to do with the poor whites of the South, who, to the
number of 100,000, represent in the single state of Virginia that accumulated and hereditary ignorance with
which Slavery curses all except a few families ; and I
have observed precisely the same arrest of development,
both physical and mental, in those poor whites.   Their
children are, in early life, of remarkable beauty ; but
they soon lose it, and become ugly, sallow, and ill-
shapen.   They learn well at first, even with a kind of
voracity ; but, at about the same age with the Negro
child, they become dull, and rarely retain in mature
age the ability to read or write, even if they have been
taught.   Then, some low tribes sell their own children
into Slavery, says Dr. Hunt.   Very bad indeed ; but it
is a thing I have known done by hundreds of whites in
Virginia.

With regard to the craniological differences between
the Negro and the white races, Dr. Hunt, knowing the
importance of the point, says and quotes much ; and, as
may be anticipated, he gives about as ugly a picture as
the celebrated one that formed the frontispiece to the
work of his Confederate brother Dr. Nott, significantly
placed by the side of a perfect love of an ape.   But,
with regard to the head and brain of the Negro, it may
be remarked, that where Tiedemann says that "the brain
of the Negro is quite as large as that of the European
and other human races," and Dr. Morton of America
says it is not ; where Dr. Hunt says it is ape-like, and
Professor Huxley that it is nearer than the heads of most
other races to the European,—it may be safely concluded
that there cannot be any such tremendous difference as

would be required to conclude that the Negro is infra-
human, much less to justify the enslavement of millions.

The writers who mask the partisan *animus* under the
noble front of science may generally be known by their
enormous suppressions of unwelcome facts; for where
simple truth is the object, every ascertained fact will
be regarded in any general statement. One who knew
nothing of the subject would suppose, in reading the
work which I am reviewing, that the Africans were a
small tribe of limited area and uniform characteristics,
and would little suspect that Europe cannot show so
many and such extreme varieties of mankind, even to
the limited extent in which we have been able to observe
them. It is a violent effort to describe as one being the
wretched Bushman and the Pangwe, of whom Wilson
declares, that of all men he has ever met, they are those
of the most noble and imposing bearing. There is much
said of the subjects of Dahomey; but why nothing of the
Kaffirs? Of them Brace says: " In person the Kaffirs
are remarkable for symmetry and beauty; their height is
usually over five feet eight inches, and their carriage is
stately and upright. Their heads are large, their forehead
being high and well developed. The hair is woolly, the
features are fine, and the eyes remarkable for their keen,
piercing expression; the nose varying in form, but sometimes of the perfect classic shape." Again, these mis-
onegrists take every low trait scattered about through
millions of people, and plant them in the face and form
of each Negro. Abundance of quotations there are also
from people who have been in Africa,—some of them, one
may fear, on very doubtful business;—but why is there
none from Livingstone? We of this generation have
some reason to associate Livingstone with trustworthy
intelligence concerning Africa. Of the inland tribes
east of Angola Livingstone writes: " All the inhabi-

tants of this region, as well as those of Londa, may be
called true Negroes, if the limitations formerly made be
borne in mind. The dark colour, thick lips, heads elon-
gated backward and upward and covered with wool,
flat noses, with other Negro peculiarities, are general;
but while these characteristics place them in the true
Negro family, the reader would imbibe a wrong idea if
he supposed that all these features combined are often
met with in one individual. All have a certain thickness and prominence of lip; but many are met with in
every village, in whom thickness and projection are not
more marked than in Europeans. All are dark; but
the colour is shaded off in different individuals from
deep black to light yellow. As we go westward, we
observe the light colour predominating over the dark;
and then again, when we come within the influence of
the damp from the sea-air, we find the shade deepen
into the general blackness of the coast population. The
shape of the head, with its woolly crop, though general,
is not universal. The tribes on the eastern side of the
continent, as the Caffres, have heads finely developed,
and strongly European. Instances of this kind are frequently seen; and often I became so familiar with the
dark colour as to forget it in viewing the countenance.
I was struck by the strong resemblance some natives
bore to certain of our own notabilities. With every disposition to pay due deference to the opinions of those
who have made ethnology their special study, I have felt
myself unable to believe that the exaggerated features
usually put forth as those of the typical Negro, character-
ise the majority of any nation of South Central Africa."

My own observations upon the Negroes of the Southern States may be summed up as follows :

The Negro child when first born is of a light choco-
late colour, and sometimes, even when its parents are

quite black, much lighter. It is only where this lightness is retained unusually long that the presence of European blood is detected. The child is, moreover, apt to be as beautiful as a child of white parents ; the thick lips, woolly hair, and other peculiarities coming later in life, just as the even more disagreeable characteristics of the so-called " poor white trash" do. But there are large numbers of very dark Negroes who have nothing but their colour and hair to distinguish them from the whites. With regard to the question which certain partisan writers in the Southern States have tried to raise concerning the continued fertility of the mixture of Negro and European blood, there is not a particle of evidence even to suggest it, but any amount to disprove it. It is extremely rare to find an instance of infertility among mulattoes, quadroons, or octoroons ; and the enormous increase of the Negroes of all hues in the South is sufficient to show that this is the case. The intimations that the descendants of these crossings are unhealthy, is disproved by the fact that the mortality among the black Negroes is greater than among the lighter ones. I do not account for this, however, by supposing that the black ones have less health, but that they oftener remain slaves than the mulattoes,—a generation of either on the plantations of the far South averaging only nine or ten years. Moreover, if those with European blood are subjected to the same hard usage and exposure, they suffer more by it than pure Negroes. The same might be said of pure Europeans, without implying that, under the usage and climate appropriate to their blood, they would be less healthy than Negroes.

With regard to the moral characteristics of the Negro, I may say, that having lived among them for many years, I have remarked that the characteristic

vices of the white races prevail as little among them as
their diseases. Their chief fault is a tendency to ignore
the distinctions of *meum* and *tuum;* but it should be remembered that the rights of property involve some very
refined problems. If the Negro is inclined to sympathise with the views of Rousseau on such questions more
than the English schools would approve, it must be admitted that the systematic disregard of his own right to
his earnings is scarcely the best method of giving him
better views. I have never heard yet of a slave who had
managed to filch back so much as had been filched from
him. Generally, however, the thefts of which so much
is said are peccadilloes committed by young Negroes,
and rarely extend beyond the abstraction of a ribbon
or some piece of finery; unless, indeed, it goes to the
flagrant excess of abstracting himself. Burglaries,
large robberies, wanton destruction (or any of the purely
vindictive crimes), are almost unknown among them.
I have known a young girl, who had stolen from her
mistress a diamond breast-pin in ignorance of its value,
restore it when she discovered the importance of the
article, though she was certain of punishment. The
universal custom in the Southern States of leaving the
white women alone with the slaves for days, and weeks
even, shows how little the Negroes are guilty of rape,
or similar crimes. I have never heard of an American
Negro's killing any one for money : the few instances
of killing that I remember in Virginia were from wrath
or jealousy, growing out of outrages perpetrated upon
the women they love by white masters. They are
morally very much superior to the whites of any country in which I have observed whites. If a Negro is
employed, he will do much not mentioned in the contract. He will never forget one who has befriended
him. He will suffer for those whom he loves. His

affections are strong and steadfast ; and he lacks selfishness to a degree that has been his undoing. Also I
should add, that the Negro has a nice sense of honour.
To this, indeed, Southern society trusts itself daily.
Every life, every babe, is in their power ; they must
be trusted at every turn with important interests and
secrets ; and they are never betrayers. One instance,
out of many that I could name, must suffice me here.
Amongst my father's slaves was one whose wife, having
become insane, was placed in a lunatic asylum in Baltimore.   The husband, who was devotedly attached to
her, was permitted to go occasionally to Baltimore to
visit her.   He was given money for the journey, and
went alone.   On each occasion he could have made good
his escape to liberty with ease ; but he invariably returned at the appointed time, and restored all the money
he had not been compelled to use.   That he did this
because he scorned to take advantage of what he regarded as my father's generosity, and not because of any
indifference to freedom, is shown in the fact, that when,
on the late approach of the United-States army, he felt
that liberty was fairly within his reach, he immediately
availed himself of it, and is now enjoying it with the
rest of whom I have to write elsewhere in these pages.

    With regard to the mental characteristics of the
Negroes in the Southern States, I have to say, that they
seem to me to be weaker in the direction of the understanding, strictly speaking, but to have strength and
elegance of imagination and expression.   Negro ser-
mons, fables, and descriptions are in the highest degree
pictorial, abounding in mystic interpretations which
would delight a German transcendentalist.   My belief
is, that there is a vast deal of high art yet to come out
of that people in America.   Their songs and hymns are
the only original melodies we have ; and one of the

finest American paintings which I have seen is a conception of Tennyson's *Lotos Eaters* painted by a Negro.
At Montecello, in Virginia, the former residence of
Thomas Jefferson, the exquisite mosaic floor, planned
and made by one of Jefferson's slaves, is yet in perfect
preservation.   The old friend of that statesman who
showed it to me said : " Mr. Jefferson always took
pleasure in showing his visitors this wonderful piece of
workmanship.   It was made by a slave, born on his
estate, who never had any instruction as a mechanic.
Mr. Jefferson always believed that the Negro race had
an important destiny."   That belief has not died away
from the leading minds of America.   That " excellent
observer," as Dr. Hunt calls him, Burmeister, said, " I
have often tried to obtain an insight into the mind of
the Negro ; but it was never worth the trouble."   Yet
in America it seems that those who have known that
race most intimately, have found in it resources and
feelings rich enough to make its story the romance of
this generation.   If the Negro has not yet the culture
to tell his own story, he has inspired the pens of Mrs.
Stowe, Epes Sargent, and many others, and has kindled
the tongues of every foremost orator.   " I esteem,"
said Ralph Waldo Emerson, " the occasion of this jubi-
lee" (West - Indian Emancipation) " to be the proud
discovery that the black race can contend with the
white ; that, in the great anthem which we call History,
a piece of many parts and vast compass, after playing
a long time a very low and subdued accompaniment,
they perceive the time arrived when they can strike in
with effect, and take a master's part in the music.   The
civility of the world has reached that pitch, that their
more moral genius is becoming indispensable ; and the
quality of this race is to be honoured for itself.   For
this they have been preserved in sandy deserts, in rice-

swamps, in kitchens and shoe-shops so long; now let them emerge, clothed, and in their own form.''

It is observable that, in the inferior orders of the world, all the marks of superiority are not to be found upon any one kind of animals; but are so distributed, that whilst a genus is higher in some one or two respects, it is at the cost of being quite inferior to other genera in other respects. Thus, illustrating by the anthropoid apes, we find that in the general conformation of the cranium the chimpanzee is highest — man being the standard; whilst in some other respects it is less like man than gorilla, orang, or some of the little *hylobates*. In the make of hand and foot, the gorilla is more manlike than any ape; in the development of cerebral hemispheres, the orang-utang is above the rest; as to face and features, the gibbon is foremost,—one species (the siamang) alone among apes having a pronounced chin. Each of these has some marked inferiorities, as decidedly beneath the simial standard itself as its advantages are above it. In fact, each would seem to be an anvil, upon which some particular part of a man is being shaped, for which other portions are, to a limited extent, in atrophy. When Man arrives, he is simply a higher order by inheriting, as the basis of his development, all those advantages which each of the lower genera had been separately fostering. Nevertheless, as man is not to be supposed to have culminated in the development of either his physical or moral nature, we shall find that he is not released from the law above stated. In the human world, also, it is easily demonstrable that each race is stronger in some direction than all others; but that for that strength it has suffered loss in other directions. One race is found with finer features and muscular tissues, another with better bone, and so on. Handsome as the European woman is, she may

well court the comparative freedom from the pains and
perils of childbirth which her swarthy sisters have.
And if we were imagining an ideal man, we should probably import his teeth from Africa, and, possibly, more
than one osteological characteristic.

It is natural that each race should estimate its own
excellence as above all excellences, it being of the first
importance that each should make perfect its own talent,
and gain its lawful usury ; it is necessary that such talent
shall be even over-estimated.   Thus, the European estimates every thing by the standard of intellect and energy.
But, after all, there is, as the world gets older, a growing appreciation of simple goodness, kindliness, and affec-
tionateness.   Intellect is the captain among the spiritual
forces ; it is brilliant, aggressive, immediately available ;
but there are quiet things, seemingly without force,
which revolutionise the world as much in the end.
Hence, if any two families of the human race should
carefully compare their leading traits, they might find
that a decision of relative merits would be very difficult.
For instance, when Dr. Hunt boasts that "the European, for ever restless, has migrated to all parts of the
world," and that "every where we see the European
as the conqueror and dominant race ;" and when he
sneers at the Negro for having been so long a slave,—one
can well fancy the President of the Gaboon Anthro-
pological Society describing the Europeans as " a people
with a passion for taking away the countries of others,
and dignifying the robbery as conquests ; with whom
satisfaction with its lot was mark of a race's inferiority ; and whose systematic brutality had been shown
for ages in chaining, buying, and selling another race."
It clearly does not occur to Dr. Hunt that there may
be on earth a mind so constituted as to sneer at the
white man because he has been an oppressor just so long

as the Negro has been a slave. By his method, the disgrace in a case of robbery is with the man weak enough to be robbed, none of it accruing to the robber. There is, it would seem, not homage, but scorn, due to him who, despised and smitten, bore it with meekness and silence.

Much has been said of late concerning the old horror of the amalgamation of the blacks and whites, as it comes in the new dress of *Miscegenation.* Of this I have a word or two to say; but first let me remind the English reader, that nobody in the Northern States has proposed that the blacks and whites shall be *compelled* to intermarry. The proposition is simply that the laws against such marriages which yet remain in some of the Northern States shall be removed. Consequently, that portion of the English press which has been so distressed on this subject may calm itself with the reflection that, were the theory of the wildest miscegenist adopted to-morrow, the relation between the blacks and whites in respect to marriage would be simply conformed to what it is in England and France to-day.

Moreover, it is well enough to remember that Miscegenation is already the irreversible fact of Southern Society in every thing but the recognition of it. Following the advice of Macheath in the *Beggar's Opera,* the Southerners have not " stood upon ceremonies ;" and consequently, although the marriage - ceremonies have been few, the mixture of blood has been very extensive. These Southerners have proved that the repulsion to the alliance of the two bloods extends only to so much of it as the parson and the magistrate have any thing to do with. Europeans often marry without hesitation darker and far less beautiful persons than the quadroon, sexteroon, or octoroon. The octoroon is generally lighter than the Spaniard or Italian.

No; the trouble is entirely in the political caste of that Negro blood : let that barrier be broken down, and there would appear a far different set of conclusions on this subject. " But," it is said, " the Abolitionists themselves are not willing to marry, or have their children marry, Negroes." No one wishes to marry, or to have a son or daughter to marry, an *unfortunate* person,—and such the American Negro is. Moreover, he is too often uncultivated. But, apart from this, the majority of Abolitionists would not object to such an alliance. Nay, let the educated Negro be introduced into America now as a learned Hindoo, or let it be a wealthy French-speaking Negro from somewhere, who shall be called Algerian, Haytian, or what not, and the Abolitionists will not be the first to seek the alliance with him. We all, in America, remember how the rich merchant of Portland was scandalised by the introduction of a Negro into an adjoining pew, until he was told that the very black man was a Haytian worth a million of money ; whereupon his wrath subsided into the gentle whisper, " Introduce me."

I, for one, am firmly persuaded that the mixture of the blacks and whites is good ; that the person so produced is, under ordinarily favourable circumstances, healthy, handsome, and intelligent. Under the best circumstances, I believe that such a combination would evolve a more complete character than the unmitigated Anglo-Saxon. The English blood has culminated as a separate power ; indeed, it would be hard to find a distinct race which has not reached or passed its solstice. But the evening-star of the epoch of separate races is the morning-star of Human Unity. Men we have ; but not yet Man. Already we know that nations are great in proportion as they are of mixed races. As in the human form and brain the long-scattered rays of force and instinct, coming up from many kingdoms, converged, so in the consummate race all races must reappear. Every race has a genius in some sort, to be unfolded by proper culture; and so long as that of the African, or any other race, however lowly, is excluded, some function will be absent from every brain, some flaw will be in every heart. To Pride and Ignorance—the twin foes of Man—many things may seem common and unclean which are quite the reverse of that. Flint is common; and yet, a little water added, you have the hydrate of silica or, noblest of all gems, the opal. How slight the difference between stove-polish and the diamond! We have not yet begun those higher combinations out of which the world's nobler offspring is to come; but Nature is full of facts and histories to remind us that the Highest is often in the Lowliest, and that the stones rejected of the builders have again and again become the Heads of the Corners — sometimes at the cost of imposing structures which had rejected those stones. Thus the whole American structure has had to be razed to the earth and rebuilt, for the sake of that one poor race rejected; not one step at reconstruction being possible until that Negro shall become the chief corner-stone. But we have not to build a Nationality on that continent; we have to rear a new Race: to this we are bound by Fate. We have already learned with some pains that the Negro is not a race that is to die out, or that can be crushed with impunity; and very near to this is the lesson that he is quite essential to the work that all races have to do on that continent, and which they cannot do until all unite as the fingers of One Great Hand.

CHAPTER X.

The Abolitionists—Their history and present attitude—
Garrison and Phillips.

" THE fate of the Negro," says Frederika Bremer, " is
the romance of our age." When the history of Negro
Emancipation in America is written, it will justify these
words. That history will tell the story of men and
women who, to win the priceless boon of freedom, have
travelled hundreds of miles clinging to the wheel-houses
of steamers, or stowed in the dark holds, or of ships
boxed up as freight, and who, in Massachusetts or
Canada, have been taken from such places half-starved,
and more like skeletons than human. beings. But History will have a nobler task than this, perhaps, in recording the devotion and sacrifices of those men of the North
who have reared the cause of the slave from its weak
and threatened infancy to its present maturity. Looking
back over the centuries to the Crusaders, led by the fire-
heart of Peter the Hermit to rescue the Holy Places of
Palestine from the infidel's tread, we are thrilled by the
devotion of men who went to their graves as to their
beds, that the sepulchre of the Holiest might become the
shrine of the believer; yet I must believe that, when
Time has given the needed perspective, the romance
which clings to those heroes of a creed will fade beside
the halo that will shine around the heads of the crusaders
in that moral struggle which has been going on for more
than thirty years in America, whose higher object has
been to rescue the Holy Places of Humanity—not the
sepulchre of Christ, but the shrine of his living presence.

The anti-Slavery movement in America has been a purely religious one. In the poor scarred slave, who sat by the way-side asking for the simplest natural rights—the merest cup of water—the right to himself, his wife, his child, these nobler crusaders recognised Him who said, " What you do or do not to the least of my brothers, you do or do not to me ;" and they started up with trimmed lamp and girt loin, and from that day have slept only upon their arms. Their history is by no means to be identified with that, noble as it is, of the brave men whose struggles have made the real history of modern Europe. These have generally been the struggles of proud races for political existence or nationality, the efforts of brave men for their own power or territory ; and as such they have kindled, as they deserved, the admiration and sympathy of all manly hearts. The Anti-Slavery Thirty Years' War in America had this quality also ; for the Slave-Power, having by the compromise of the fathers an over-balance of representation, and by the invention of the cotton-gin a vast accession of wealth, had been able to buy up the leading pulpits and presses of the North, and to subsidise her leading statesmen, and thus to wield over the whole country the tyranny of an autocracy. But in two or three regards the flag of the Abolitionists was nobler than that under which revolutionists of other lands marched. In the first place, they were struggling for a real " idea," namely, the right of every man to himself,—an idea unconfined to their own country in its importance, and one which they placed so high above any mere question of nationality, that, for the sake of that idea, they arrayed themselves against their country's unity. No question of the unity of this land, or the ancient boundaries of that, can, however important, be regarded as equal to that which rests upon the sacredness of Man,

which vaults above all nationalities. In the second
place, these men were banded together and making the
greatest sacrifices for this idea, where its denial pressed
upon *a race not their own;* and their cause demanded
that they should renounce voting, or the holding of any
office of profit or honour, and indeed all political privileges, as completely as they were denied to the race they
befriended,—that they should literally remember those
who were bound as bound with them. In the third
place, they rejected all weapons except the legitimate
ones of Civilisation and Humanity. The entrenchments
of the great injustice were attacked with arrows of light;
every fuse was lighted only by the fire of convinced
and devoted hearts. They counselled no violence; they
relied upon the power of truth and right, and never
doubted the victory—which seemed, however, painfully
distant. The Abolitionists were the original revolutionists; though their revolution was so purely Christian,
so in keeping with the higher spirit of the age and of
the New World, that those who took up the legitimate
weapons of the Past and its wrongs to suppress that
noble revolution, are spoken of as the revolutionists.
The Secessionists represent the Union as it was, and are
fighting to reestablish that which the Abolitionists have
overthrown,—to perpetuate things as they were before
the election of Abraham Lincoln announced the new
order.

The pioneer of the anti-Slavery movement was William Lloyd Garrison. It was about thirty-three years
ago, when he was editing a paper in Baltimore, Maryland, that the sale and shipment of some slaves at that
city for the New-Orleans market excited his indignation,
and he bitterly denounced it in his journal as an outrage
against Christianity. He was thrown into prison because he could not pay a heavy sum declared at his trial

to be a suitable indemnity to the aggrieved merchants who shipped the Negroes, and whom, it was decided, he had grossly libelled. A gentleman of New York paid the money; and Garrison went to New England, resolved to devote himself from that moment to the abolition of Slavery. He was a member in high standing of the Baptist denomination, and at once tried to enlist in his cause the ministers of the Gospel in Boston; but they gave him a cold reception. He could not get a church, nor even a vestry-room, in which to discuss Slavery. There was, however, a hall in Boston, hitherto used only for the meetings of freethinkers; these infidels came forward and offered him the use of their hall. So this highest phase of American religion began in the lowly manger of an infidel debating-room. Yet there were not wanting a few who, having watched their flocks in the general night, at length came forward to lay their gifts at the feet of the infant cause of Humanity —chief among whom were Dr. Follen, S. J. May, and (though later) Dr. Channing, all clergymen of high repute in the Unitarian Society; a society which should be credited for a singular fidelity in its opposition to Slavery, and which has on that account never been able to sustain a church farther south than Washington, though it has in Richmond, Charleston, Mobile, and New Orleans church-buildings, whose closed doors and silent pulpits are eloquent testimonies against the wrong which could not bear discussion, and monuments to the courage of the Church which would never, except in isolated cases, bow to that Baal. I do not sympathise with the ordinarily recognised Unitarian interpretation of Christianity, but feel bound to give the above credit to those to whom it is due, and to say that Southerners unanimously regard it as a radically anti-Slavery Church.

But the common people heard Garrison gladly; and

G

he soon had to adjourn his meetings from the infidels'
little hall to the open Boston Common.

On the first day of January 1831, he began the
publication of a weekly paper, *The Liberator*.   He had
no money, and he joined himself to a man who had just
the same capital ; but they managed to get a small attic
room, with a Negro boy to help them, and set up the
types for their paper with their own hands.   I have
looked with profound interest over the first number of
The Liberator.   It is a small single sheet, about eight
inches by twelve to the page.   It is opened with these
words, signed with Garrison's name : *" I am in earnest ;
I will not equivocate, I will not excuse, I will not re-
treat a single inch ; and I will be heard."*   It was not
many years before the Slave-Power felt in this paper
the first shudder of a coming earthquake; and the Governor of South Carolina called upon the Governor of
Massachusetts to suppress it.   Edward Everett, then
Governor of Massachusetts, and always the willing tool
of the Slave-Power until now (the " ever strong upon
the stronger side"), sent a committee to find Garrison ;
and when they had reported the lowliness and poverty
of *The Liberator* concern, Mr. Everett wrote to the Governor of South Carolina, that the party he inquired
after was of no social or other importance, and that
Massachusetts would take care that no insult should be
allowed against Southern institutions.   But vainly does
the dog assure the mouse of the peaceful disposition of
the cat: Slavery had an instinct wiser than Everett, and
set a price on the head of Garrison, by laws passed in
several of the Southern legislatures.   And yet *The Liberator* went on, and from being so small grew large
enough to be what it is to-day,—the winding-sheet of
Slavery.*

* For the fullest account of the rise and progress of the

Though Garrison is the pioneer of the radical anti-
Slavery movement, Wendell Phillips must be regarded
as its representative man. When, as a young and
accomplished gentleman and lawyer, he was regarded
with pride by the wealthy and aristocratic society of
Boston to which he belonged, there was no dream of
his subsequent career in his mind ; perhaps he saw, as
the leading men of Boston saw, his path paved all the
way to the White House. Certainly there was no position of eminence which his position and talents might
not have commanded, had he shared the apathy of those
about him to the fate of the slave. Young Phillips was
betrothed to a woman of superior qualities, and she persuaded him to go one evening to hear the anti-Slavery
agitator. He heard a strong appeal in behalf of simple justice. He did not go away sorrowful because of his great
possessions, but went away to think. Soon afterwards,
when there was a large meeting held in the city to consider the murder of the Illinois editor Lovejoy, who had
been shot by a mob because he denounced the burning of
a Negro at St. Louis, and the meeting was on the point of
being carried by various distinguished men for Slavery,
Phillips arose, and with burning words, which fired the
people, carried through strong resolutions against Slavery and its latest crime. When the meeting was over,
Garrison met the young orator at the door and clasped
hands with him ; and those hands were never unclasped
again. Side by side they have fought the battle up to
this hour of its victory. The news sped through the
city that the most promising young lawyer of Boston
had joined with the vulgar Abolitionists : many disbe-

anti-Slavery movement in America, and many interesting anec-
dotes connected therewith, the reader is referred to Harriet
Martineau's " Martyr Age of the United States," *London and
Westminster Review*, vol. xxxii. no. 1.

lieved it, and many besought him to retrace the step;
but the knight had buckled on his armour, and received
from the divine hand his trusty sword ; and from that
time has been seen, like the white plume of Navarre,
always in the thick of the conflict.

Few scenes are so impressive as Wendell Phillips
before the crowds which, in vast numbers, flock to hear
him in the American cities.   At his first imperial glance
every eye is intent; and from his first sentence every
mind is spell - bound.   The speaker stands before his
audience with the air of a man set there by destiny
for a certain work, and bearing in his brain the full
repository of weapons necessary for that work.   A
model of manly beauty, with a most noble presence, a
fair complexion, a blue eye full of light, he is recognised at once as the authorised messenger of high principles ; whilst his calm and chaste eloquence is doubled
in power by the fact that the people know what the
man surrendered for those principles, and see, as the
platform on which he stands, all the common ambitions
underfoot of the soul they could not conquer.

The Garrisonians stood aloof from the political world;
but by their influence they had created a political party,
which was related to them as the present opposition
party of the *Corps Législatif* of France is related to
Ledru Rollin and his compatriots, who will not touch
the Empire by the holding of any office which requires
an oath of allegiance to it at the threshold.   This party,
the Republican, is the child of the anti-Slavery movement.   When I first became attracted to the ranks of
the Abolitionists, about twelve years ago, I found that
there were many varieties of opinion among them as to
method.   Gerritt Smith, Foster, and others, believed
that Congress had the right to abolish Slavery.   Mr.
Seward and Mr. Sumner believed that the Government

was to be so reformed that it would be administered in
the interest of Freedom, and that this would finally give
such an anti - Slavery education to the people, that at
length a Convention would be called, which, with the
requisite majority of three-fourths of the States, would
amend the Constitution with a clause abolishing Slavery.
Theodore Parker firmly believed that Slavery would go
down in blood, and that the North should prepare for
war.   In 1853 I heard him prophesy that the second
presidential election from that time would be followed
by war.   The Abolitionists of the Garrison school were
convinced that the Union should and would be divided ;
and that this, by bringing the safe refuge of the slave
from Canada down to the very doors of Slavery, would
be followed by a general escapade of the slaves.

When the Southern States passed ordinances of
secession, the Abolitionists saw the consummation of
one phase of their work drawing nigh, and generally
advocated the policy of permitting those States to de-
part ; they were ready, indeed, to build them a bridge
of gold by which to leave.   Of course they did not
dream of laying down their arms, but knew that they
could the better fight against Slavery when their own
country had no complicity with it, and no one could
claim that any compromise with it was a patriotic duty.
Theodore Parker had, indeed, always opposed the disunion policy of the Abolitionists, as putting the oppression of the slaves beyond the power of the North.
The real difference between him and the Garrisonian
school was, that Mr. Parker had a strong faith, which
the others had not, that the North was at heart anti-
Slavery, and would presently rise to put down Slavery.
Garrison believed that no healthy action of the popular
heart could be obtained till the idol Union was shattered.
When, therefore, the Southern States seceded, the Abo-

litionists regarded that as the best bargain they could
secure, though they knew as well as others the illegality
of the Southern movement.   (They themselves had
never contemplated disunion except through the constitutional method of a Convention of the States.)   The
spirit of compromise was, at that time, exasperated to
the utmost; and there was great reason to fear that the
South was not sufficiently in earnest, but was only
making a desperate demand for further guarantees to
Slavery, in which case the Union might have been re-
constructed over the crushed form of the slave.   But
when the South made an armed attack upon the Government, and the nation took up the gauntlet thrown
down at Sumter, and rose *en masse* with the highest
enthusiasm to sustain the Government, not only did the
phantom of a reconstruction on the basis of Slavery fade
away, but in its place a power was unsealed—the War
Power—which would, if pressed to the utmost, as they
knew it must be, give the Abolitionists a boon far beyond their anticipations, and secure thirty-four States
for Liberty instead of fifteen.

So late as the 20th of January 1861, Wendell Phillips concluded an oration on Disunion in the Boston
Music Hall, long the pulpit of Parker, with these words:
" All hail, Disunion !   Beautiful on the mountains are
the feet of him that bringeth good tidings, that pub-
lisheth peace, that saith unto Zion, Thy God reigneth.
The sods of Bunker Hill shall be greener now that their
great purpose is accomplished.   Sleep in peace, martyr
of Harper's Ferry ! your life was not given in vain.
Rejoice, spirits of Fayette and Kosciusko ! the only
stain upon your swords is passing away.   Soon, throughout all America, there shall be neither wish nor power
to own a slave."

On the 21st of April in that year, Mr. Phillips stood

upon the same platform, now decorated with the stars and stripes, and said : " Many times this winter, here and elsewhere, I have counselled peace,—urged, as well as I knew how, the expediency of acknowledging a Southern Confederacy, and the peaceful separation of these thirty-four States. One of the journals announces to you that I come here this morning to retract those opinions. No ; not one word of them ! I need them all,—every word I have spoken this winter,—every act of twenty-five years of my life,—to make the welcome I give this war hearty and hot. Civil war is a momentous evil. It needs the soundest, most solemn justification. I rejoice before God to-day for every word that I have spoken counselling peace ; but I rejoice also with an especially profound gratitude, that now, the first time in my anti-Slavery life, I speak under the stars and stripes, and welcome the tread of Massachusetts men marshalled for war. No matter what the Past has been or said ; to-day the slave asks God for a sight of this banner, and counts it the pledge of his redemption. Hitherto it may have meant what you thought, or what I thought ; to-day it represents sovereignty and justice. *The only mistake that I have made was in supposing Massachusetts wholly choked with cotton-dust and cankered with gold.* The South thought her patience and general willingness for peace, cowardice ; to-day shows her mistake. She has been sleeping on her arms since '83, and the first cannon-shot brings her to her feet with the war-cry of the Revolution on her lips. Any man who loves either liberty or justice must rejoice at such an hour."

It will thus be seen that the attitude of the Abolitionists in this war is perfectly comprehensible and consistent. They had sought disunion ; but it was not a geographical disunion they sought : they aimed only to

free themselves and their country from complicity with
Slavery, of which the Union, so long as the South prevailed in it, was a seal. As far as they had aimed to
destroy it, the Union was destroyed ; any Union with
Slavery in it was henceforth impossible. The emancipation they had pursued under the form of Disunion,
henceforth became identified with Union; and they now
strive for this with the same singleness with which they
had striven for the other, until that first of their labours
was crowned with success. That the Abolitionists have
never, in the excitement of the conflict, lost sight of the
first and highest object to which they were consecrated,
may be known from the fact, that when the present Administration has seemed, at various times, inclined to
conduct the war without reference to the freedom of the
slaves, they have boldly prayed for defeat. " Let us
hope," said Mr. Phillips, " that Southern success may
be so rapid and abundant, that a blow like that which
stuns the drunkard into sobriety may stun our Cabinet
into vigour, and that nineteen millions of people, putting forth their real strength in the right direction, may
keep peace outside our borders until we make peace
within."

That the Abolitionists unanimously recognise in this
war purely a struggle between Slavery and Freedom,
should be a sufficient guarantee to the lovers of Freedom throughout the world of the nature of the war.
Little heed need be given to those who speak of other
issues, when such representative States as Massachusetts and South Carolina agree and frankly declare that
it is a war on the simple issue of Slavery.

CHAPTER XI.

Secession illegal—Effected by violence and dishonesty—How
Virginia seceded.

SOON after the Secession Ordinance of South Carolina
was passed, and when President Buchanan had announced that he could not find any authority in the
Constitution to coerce a State, the London *Times* (Jan.
9, 1861) had an editorial article of great ability, the
opening sentences of which are as follows: " Never for
many years can the United States be to the world what
they have been. Mr. Buchanan's Message has been a
greater blow to the American people than all the rants
of the Georgian Governor or the ' Ordinances' of the
Charleston Convention. The President has dissipated
the idea that the States which elected him constitute one
people. We had thought that the Federation was of
the nature of a nationality; we find it nothing more
than a partnership. If any State may, on grounds satis-
factory to a local Convention, dissolve the union between
itself and its fellows ; if discontent with the election of
a president, or the passing of an obnoxious law by another State, or, it may be, a restrictive tariff, gives a
State the ' right of revolution,' and permits it to with-
draw itself from the community,—then the position of
the American people with respect to foreign powers is
completely altered."

No rational man can doubt the justice of these remarks. If the investments in public works, in railways
and canals, for example, running through many States,
which have been constantly invited and received from
foreign capitalists, had been understood to be in a go-

vernment which could not protect or vouch for the various segments of such works in this or that State, the values of stocks would have been materially altered. Every treaty or business arrangement between other nations and the United States would have been different, had it been given out that that Government was bound only by a rope of sand, which the coal interest, or the cotton interest, or other local interest, might crumble with a touch. Nor would the differences have been less in the dealings between the States themselves. Some railways in the far West, and even some cities,—*e. g.* Chicago,— are almost *owned* in New York and Boston by men and companies who certainly supposed that the regions in which they invested money were permanent portions of the United States.

The Northern people have decided with unanimity that, in giving to the world such an opinion, Buchanan betrayed his trust. And their position is very simple:

The first Confederation of the States was made as a military rather than a civil measure: it was meant to band together the States, so as to make England afraid to attempt a subjugation of her revolted colonies. Those Articles of Confederation declared that the States should be sovereign. Yet they specially provided that the Union so made should be *perpetual,* and their official title was, "Articles of Confederation and *Perpetual* Union."

After a few years it was found that the government so made was very loose; as the fear of English invasion was laid, the military confederation was proved insufficient for a civil government. Hence the States formed a Convention, which made what was officially called " a more perfect Union."

It certainly could not have been a more perfect Union if the element of "perpetuity," distinctly existing even in the loose Confederation, were omitted in the Federation.

SUPREMACY OF THE CONSTITUTION. 91

In the next place, whereas the first Articles had
been between the States, this is between the People of
all the States, beginning, " We, the People," &c.

This Constitution was accepted and ratified by all the
States without any conditions whatever. And, by adopting it, the States transferred their sovereignty to the
united voice of the People of the United States.

In the State of Virginia, Patrick Henry, Mr. Gra-
ham, and others, vehemently opposed the adoption of
the Constitution, on the ground that it took away the
State supremacy. There were large minorities in several States against the ratification, all upon the same
correct and recognised ground. The leaders of the
Southern movement have repeatedly spoken of the
great *reluctance* with which some States adopted that
Constitution. Why this reluctance? It would not be
natural that there should be any great reluctance for a
State or a man to enter into a contract which might be
broken at their pleasure,—the next day or moment.
That reluctance confessed that they saw in the obligation
the surrender of their sovereignty and the element of
permanency. And truly it did not require much sa-
gacity to see as much in a Constitution whose sixth
Article declared, " This Constitution, and the laws of the
United States which shall be made in pursuance thereof,
and all treaties made, or which shall be made, under the
authority of the United States, shall be the supreme law
of the land; and the judges in every State shall be
bound thereby, any thing in the Constitution or laws of
any State to the contrary notwithstanding."

The greatest of the Southerners, Mr. Calhoun, in a
Declaration of Principles for South Carolina, drawn up
by him in 1828, distinctly declares that the State had,
by adopting the Federal Constitution, " modified its
original right of sovereignty, whereby its individual

consent was necessary to any change in its political condition, and, by becoming a member of the Union, had placed that power in the hands of three-fourths of the States (the number necessary for a Constitutional amendment), in whom the highest power known to the Constitution actually resides."

It has been vaguely asserted that the State of Virginia, when it ratified the Constitution, reserved the right of resuming its sovereignty. This is not the case. The preamble to the Virginia ratification says : " We, the delegates of the people of Virginia, duly elected, &c., do, in the name and in behalf of the people of Virginia, declare and make known, that the powers granted under the Constitution, being derived from THE PEOPLE OF THE UNITED STATES, may be resumed BY THEM." The position stated here is unquestionable. There is no doubt that the Union may be destroyed by the same power that made it ; that three-fourths of the States in a Convention might restore to each State its sovereignty. When, in March 1861, Messrs. Forsyth and Crawford were in Washington as Confederate Commissioners, the Secretary of State wrote to them that he was " prevented altogether from admitting or assuming that the States referred to by them have, in law or in fact, withdrawn from the Federal Union, or that they could do so in the manner described by Messrs. Forsyth and Crawford, or in any other manner than with the consent and concert of the people of the United States, to be given through a National Convention to be assembled in conformity with the provisions of the Constitution." In this he did but stand upon the principle above quoted from the great partisan leader of the South, John C. Calhoun.

Attempts have been made to set aside the force of these facts by alleging that the Northern States, or some of them, had violated their part of the contract in the Constitution, reference being made to what are known as the Personal Liberty Bills, by which certain States have made the pursuit of fugitive slaves less easy within their borders than before. But if these humane laws were unconstitutional, there was an appointed tribunal before which they could be arraigned. The States had all agreed to abide by the decisions of the United States Supreme Court, which was created to consider such questions as these. The South could not have had any fear of coming before that Court with such a question, as the judges were chiefly Southern by birth, and all, save one, of pro-Slavery sympathies. There could be no reason for their not coming before this Court if they had had any case. By the terms of the contract, every State law must be supposed constitutional until that Court has decided otherwise.

The South, therefore, must rest absolutely upon the right of revolution. But here it was not willing to stand ; for the people of the South were not ready, with their leaders, to revolutionise against the Union. Certain forms must be gone through in order that the masses should have a vague impression that the United States was overthrowing the organic law in suppressing rebellion. The Secessionists would have been outvoted in a Constitutional Convention ; they would have been met by a powerful opposition at home, had they taken to open revolution ; so they, by State Conventions and Legislatures, passed ordinances of secession. How dishonest all this was, and how unworthy of true and brave revolutionists, may be estimated by the fact, that every regular governor, judge, legislator, or other State officer who assisted in secession, *had sworn to support the Constitution of the United States as a condition essential to entering upon his office,—each empowered for his disloyal work by a solemn oath of allegiance to the United States.*

Mr. Toombs, then a Senator at Washington from Georgia, said, " Gentlemen alone make revolutions; the lower classes are always the last to come into them." There is no doubt that the masses of the South required much forcing before they took up arms against the United States. When I was a Secessionist in Virginia, I remember well that though the majority were pro-Slavery, it was but a small minority who met in private clubs to devise means for undermining the Union. For many years the Southerners, who held the keys of every Department at Washington, were preparing secretly for the grand *coup-d'état*. The correspondence of Jefferson Davis, captured by United-States soldiers in Mississippi, shows that when he was in the War Department, a sworn constitutional adviser of the Government, he was treacherously arming the Southern section of the country and disarming the North. My uncle, Judge Eustace Conway, for some years a member of the Legislature of Virginia, was a member of the Cincinnati Convention which nominated Mr. Buchanan for President, and said within my hearing, on the day after his return, that he and other Southern delegates to that Convention had not consented to vote for Buchanan until they had received from him a solemn pledge that, in any issue that might occur between the North and the South, he —Buchanan—would take the side of the South; a pledge which he literally fulfilled. This scheming had been going on a long time. Mr. Thomas Carlyle has informed me, that soon after the publication of his first pro-Slavery pamphlet, nearly fifteen years ago, he had received letters from many leading Southerners gratefully acknowledging his work in their behalf, and welcoming it as an indication of the return of England to Slavery ; and saying, that if England could be induced to restore Slavery in the West Indies, they, the Southerners, would promise to cut loose from the North and reunite with the English Government.

I know well, from near relatives who were then in Virginia, how that State was thrown into the scale of rebellion. When South Carolina seceded, there was found to be a large majority in the State of Virginia averse to following her lead. At this time a secret Convention of secession leaders was held in Richmond, where it was decided that Virginia must be ranged with South Carolina, though by force. The plan was, that in some way an act of war against the United States should be committed ; and that when this was followed by the natural retaliation, the South would be instantly subjected to a military dictatorship and martial law, under which circumstances any proposition for balloting could easily be overborne.

The hesitation of South Carolina to begin war gave the people time to elect a Convention, in which, when it met at Richmond, there was found to be a large majority against secession. Then South Carolina was visited by a committee, which informed her that nothing could be done with Virginia until there was a collision ; whereupon South Carolina determined to fire upon Fort Sumter. When President Lincoln, in pursuance of his oath to maintain the laws, called for seventy-five thousand men to defend the country, the cry of " The South invaded !" was raised, the opponents of secession in the Virginia Convention were browbeaten and insulted ; and when many had thus been forced to yield, the rest had pistols drawn upon them, and were told that they must vote for the ordinance of secession, or take the consequences of joining with Yankees against Southerners. When these delegates returned home, they had still hard work to snap the ties which bound the unpolitical masses to the Union. At the courthouse of my native county, Stafford, a meeting was called to ratify the secession of the State, and the struggle was terrible; and when at last one, who had been a delegate at Richmond, and opposed secession as long as it was possible, arose and told the people that it was too late for resistance to the ordinance, the crowd sobbed and groaned with pain.

The Secessionists frequently appeal to the early declaration of our fathers, that all just government derives its power from the consent of the people governed, as one which the North is violating in its attempt to subdue the South. In the beginning of the rebellion, the London *Times* remarked that it was amusing to hear a person quoting the Declaration of Independence to support his right to take his slaves where he wished. But the above facts will show that it is even more audacious than amusing. That the South would not agree to the proposition to submit their cause to a Convention of the people, shows that they had no faith that they could get a majority for disunion in their States: they could not have feared the non-consent of the North, *for at that time not one public man of the North had declared for the coercion of the South, and the leading men had declared in favour of peaceable secession, if the South was, with any show of unanimity, determined to go.* For this every leading pulpit and every newspaper had declared. The subsequent proceedings of the Southern leaders convinced all that there was a large element of Southern society which had been drawn into secession by force; and when to this was added the four millions of slaves,—held down by a power which had never asked " the consent of those governed,"—it was recognised that the invasion of the South was really the liberation of its people.

It will be seen, then, that every step of the South has been marked by perjury, treachery, and lawlessness. In fact, I have been long convinced that there is nothing in

the South which can justly be called " society." There
is there a formulised anarchy, an organic disorder,
which is a rudimentary society, but that is all. The lawlessness and violence of the secession movement were
not, however, at all abnormal. Slavery is war in its
chronic form. The violence which it now shows is but
an exasperated condition of the South, as we who have
lived there have always known it. Its nightly patrols,
its duels, its constant recourse to pistols and bowie-
knives, its suspension of all the forms of law when an
Abolitionist or an insubordinate slave is to be disposed
of, its Lynch-law,—all these things have long marked
the life of that institution which war first created, and
which, having always relied upon brute force as its central
condition of existence, has, in bringing on a civil war,
only resorted to its legitimate weapons.

Let those who express so much horror of war remember that the worst kind of war is that of the strong
against the weak,—the armed against the defenceless;
the war of the South carried on from generation to
generation against unarmed men, against women and
children, has at last brought on her that calamity which
never fails to attend the " heritage of triumphant wrong."

How plain, indeed, may be seen at every stage of
this American war the retributive fires rained down from
the inviolable laws which sustain the universe! The
North has suffered only less than the South, and it was
only less guilty than the South. The region which has
been most desolated has been that slave-breeding belt
through the Border States, where the cruelest and basest
crimes of Slavery were wrought in furnishing slaves for
the markets of the far South—the region that might be
named " the middle passage" of the South. And amidst
these terrible flames, he has walked the most unscathed
who was the most innocent—the Negro.

H

CHAPTER XII.

The comparative treatment of Negroes in the North and in the
South—The origin of anti-Negro sentiment—Mobs—The
growth of better principles.

NOTHING has more astonished me in England than
the assertion so frequently made, that the Negro is more
despised and maltreated in the North than in the South.
A statement so obviously improbable could hardly have
received serious attention, had it not been for its exceedingly paradoxical nature; for it is surely startling enough
to attract attention when persons, apparently well informed, affirm that men and women are better off in
a region where they have no political or legal rights—
where they are slaves—than in a region where they
have every legal equality and many political privileges.
As this statement is, however, earnestly and widely
made, and as it has a seeming confirmation in the anti-
Negro mobs which have disgraced certain portions of
the North, I will refer briefly to it.

I have before mentioned that the wrongs of the
Negro in the South have from time to time excited the
indignation even of Southerners. They are not allowed
any intellectual instruction whatever. Their family relations are unprotected, and the *home* is unknown to
them. The husband and parent have no protection from
the enforced prostitution of the wife and child in law;
and the accordant facts are, that families are almost sure
to be separated, and that nearly every slave woman is
brutally used. I have never known of a Negro woman,
married or unmarried, who passed her life without becoming a mother. Each year that brings no increase from the

female slave is one of direct pecuniary loss to the owner;
and of the female fugitives from the South, it is well
known that the vast majority have fled because of such
brutal usage. If a male relative has resisted such treatment of a Negro woman, the law punishes it as simple
insubordination, without inquiry into the provocation.

When I first reached Massachusetts, I carefully visited
the Negro quarters of Boston; during my first summer
there, I visited those of Canada; and for many years I
was familiar with the coloured population of Cincinnati;
and in all these places I found the Negroes possessing,
for the most part, comfortable homes, their children
attending the public schools, either with the whites, or,
if prejudices against that still lingered, special schools
prepared by the State for them. That they were in most
of the Northern States a caste, a people by themselves,
was true; but it was equally true of the Irish; and it is
impossible for a candid mind to compare this mere social
inferiority with their condition in the South, where the
same social inferiority existed in a greater degree, with
the deprivation of all legal and political privileges, and
the right to education, superadded. So much common-
sense might judge from the great number of fugitives to
the North, not one of whom was ever known to return
to Slavery. So much the South confessed in the importance it attached to a Fugitive - Slave Law, which so
attractive a system, as some allege Slavery to be, could
scarcely have required.* Nevertheless, I would not stand
between the Northern communities, where Negroes have
been subjected to prejudices and indignities, and any re-
buke that should be given in the interest of the wronged
Negro, and not in the interest of those who would wrong

* Mr. Jefferson Davis gives a notable comment on the
attractiveness and benignancy of Slavery to the slave, in his
recent proposition that the slaves employed in Confederate
service shall be liberated "*as the reward* of faithful services."

him more deeply.   Yet I would earnestly call attention to the fact, that this prejudice and these wrongs have been the surplus fruit of Slavery itself.   It was because the Negroes were slaves at the South that they were an inferior caste in the North, and in proportion as any community was hostile to Slavery this prejudice disappeared ; as, for example, in Massachusetts, where the Negroes attend the public schools of all grades with whites, vote, and have every social privilege that, as in the case of whites, their talents or attainments naturally reach. Moreover, I affirm *that there never was any indignity or violence offered the Negroes in the North at any point except by the direct instigation of Slavery when that institution demanded it.*   In times when Slavery was pressing some point for its own advantage, and only then, it has shown that it could bribe certain of its tools in the North, or send up its agents, to instigate violence against Negroes. This has always been done by working upon the fears of the more ignorant Irishmen, by suggesting that the Negroes, by becoming free and coming from South to North, would take away much of their employment.   Every Negro mob has been an Irish mob.   And every one, I repeat, will be found indicating its origin in Southern Slavery by its historical association with some important emergency of Slavery.

And as this Northern prejudice originated with, and depended for its life upon, Slavery, it has been swiftly departing during this war with the strength of Slavery. The last great mob in New York against the Negroes was doubtless the last that can ever occur, and was simply one of the death-agonies of the base spirit which Slavery had engendered in the North.   If it was notable for being a manifestation of pro-Slavery feeling yet strong in New York, it proved the occasion of a still more notable manifestation of the radical reformation of the people on that subject ; for never before was a

wronged class so amply remunerated, not only by the
greatest possible compensation for its losses, but by the
affectionate sympathy of thousands who had hitherto
shared the prejudice against Negroes, but now visited
them and ministered to them.   It is, indeed, the unanimous opinion of the people of New York, that the mob
itself was an effort to stem the mighty current of repent-
ance towards that unfortunate class then showing itself
in many ways.   Its effect has been, of course, to increase the beneficent change.   Negroes are now allowed
a free entrance into the street-cars and railway-carriages
of every Free State, with possibly one single exception—
a street-car in New York.   Two years ago I saw several
Negroes and several members of the Cabinet riding in a
public carriage together at Washington, within a few
rods from the spot where I had formerly known Negroes
displayed for sale.

I shall have elsewhere to recur to the indications of
a national regeneration, inaugurated, though far from
complete, in America, as expressed in many facts; and
I will only add here, that the importance of these indications is chiefly the evidence they give of the growth of
a nobler people in America.   Whatever changes have
occurred, have come from the popular heart.   President
Lincoln has, in a recent letter to Mr. Hodges, of Kentucky, called him and the Border States to note that not
he but " events" have attacked Slavery : he confesses
that his principle was to touch Slavery last of all, and then
as lightly as possible ; but " events" dragged him on.   I
grieve, in one sense, to affirm that he uttered the truth :
to this moment he shields the actual conditions of
Southern society as much as he can—to our grievous
cost ; but at the same time the confession affords a
ground of hope ; for these " events," which proved over-
strong for the slow Kentuckian President, can and do
mean nothing else than the overwhelming determination

of the American people that Slavery shall be utterly destroyed. And, moreover, it cannot be said that this determination is merely the result of the war, and the dictate of expediency or momentary anger. We have the authority of every Southern leader and seceding State for claiming that the war is the result of this growth of Northern principle. In the face of every threat of disunion Mr. Lincoln was elected,— avowedly because he promised that he would " deal with Slavery AS WRONG." The South has itself borne witness that the growth of feeling in the North on this subject was such as to threaten her institutions. The popular love of Liberty in the North *caused* the war before it was increased, as it certainly has been, *by* the war.

In the gardens of a European palace there is a dial with a small cannon attached. When the sun rises to its meridian height, the cannon is fired, a sun-glass having been so arranged as to concentrate the rays for that purpose. Not far from this is another dial, arranged like that made by Linnæus at Upsal, in which the hours are marked by the closing of some flowers and the unfolding of others. The cannon's roar in America to-day proclaims Liberty in the ascendant : America was assailed at Fort Sumter only for turning her face towards that sunrise. The movements on the battle-field all observe ; but beyond that there lies in America another realm, in which the advancing light is traced in the closing up of old wrongs and the unfolding of high truths and principles. The false peace that covered a lie, the disposition to compromise with the injustice, have already closed ; the prejudice against the Negro is closing, and by that light devotion to liberty unfolds. And I believe that the hour is not far distant when the suffering, unfaltering people of America shall see closing together the twin, blood-stained growths, War and Slavery, and the fair flowers, Justice and Peace, expanding beyond.

CHAPTER XIII.

The parted sea—Escape of my father's slaves—Their success
under freedom.

BEFORE the war broke out I had been secretly addressed
with the question from some Negroes in and around my
old home in Virginia: How can we get free? I was afraid
to give any advice, for I knew that, as things then were,
the attempt of any slave to escape, if unsuccessful, might
result in his death; and if not that, would certainly result in his being borne to the far South, the slave's Tar-
tarus. The time had been when I would have laid the
matter before my father; but of late years I had learned
with pain that he had abandoned his old moderation on
the Slavery question, and become a warm advocate of
the system. I was compelled to say to the slaves who
had appealed to me, that I could give them no advice,
but that if I should ever meet any of them in Cincinnati,
where I resided, I would do my best to place them beyond the reach of danger. When the war broke out,
and raged all around Fredericksburg, I expected to meet
with some of these slaves. At length—it was about
sixteen months ago—I received a note from my sister,
who had married a Northern gentleman, saying that one
of my father's slaves had been seen in Washington City.
I instantly left Cincinnati, and, after travelling without
pause two days and a night, arrived at the capital, and
began to search for the contraband. I began the search
in Georgetown,—a town adjoining Washington,—where
were chiefly the quarters of newly-escaped Negroes.
I made poor headway on the first day, owing to the

suspicion which was attached by the Negroes to every
white man who sought one of their number; for kid-
napping had not even then ceased in the District.   To
one and another I went up and said, " Do you know any
thing of a coloured man about here named Dunmore?"
The persons addressed would stare as vacantly as Mr.
Weller when called on to pick out his father in the
court-room, and invariably had never heard of any such
man.   I soon suspected the point of the difficulty, and
on the next day came in company with a well-known
coloured man, when I found that the same Negroes had
suddenly acquired a fund of information concerning
Dunmore, whom I soon discovered.   He had been living
at Georgetown nearly a month, with his wife, daughter,
and her infant child.   These people had not, for their
part, quite sustained the prophecies of helplessness and
suffering so glibly made concerning emancipated Negroes; they had set up a small cake-and-candy store,
taken in washing, and managed, quite illogically, to get
a comfortable home in their few weeks of freedom, and
to save up in money more than $60.   And having taken
pains to search into the matter, I found that the contrabands around them were doing quite as well.

Dunmore told me that the rest of my father's slaves
were also free, with the exception of those who had been
hired at Richmond and other places beyond the reach of
the military lines of the United States.   My father, who,
as I have said, was the kindest of masters, had no idea
that any slave of his desired freedom.   In the spring he
had written to us in the North: " The Northerners will
see that these Negroes, instead of going to them, will
remain loyally at our side through this ordeal."   It was
but a few days after he wrote this that General McDowell
unfurled the stars and stripes over Falmouth, and that
every slave of that region, my father's included, was

under it asking for freedom. Amongst them was the
man of whom I have spoken elsewhere as having had
several times the opportunity of gaining his freedom,
when he went by consent to see his insane wife at Baltimore; and there were aged persons, for whose comfort
every provision had been made and no labour expected,
who were determined that to die free were better than to
live comfortably as slaves. They came, when they found
they could do so with safety, and took leave of my
parents with tears; but their resolution did not melt
with their hearts. Amongst the many slaves who were
liberated by General McDowell at the same time, were all
that remained of the slaves of the Chatham estate, who
had been robbed by Lacy, and laws made for such as
he, of their freedom, as I have elsewhere related. This
miscreant had, however, sold almost all the youngest
of the ninety-five slaves so wronged to the far South,
through sheer fear of living on his farm with them
after his crime. Nevertheless nearly twenty of his slaves
were set free, and saw him brought, in the trappings of
a major, a prisoner to his former home, then the head-
quarters of General McDowell. This Lacy, the man
most marked by all the slaves of that region, passed
through a large crowd of those who had lately been
owned by himself and his neighbours, his hands tied,
his head hung down; and yet not one jeering word or
imprecation was flung at him by those he had wronged.

These Negroes when liberated at once began working for the soldiers, in order to make some money
with which to go with their families to a more secure
region. When I met Dunmore, he told me that the rest
were still working thus at Falmouth. Having some
reason to believe that Falmouth would soon be evacuated
by our troops, and that these Negroes might fall again
into the hands of Slavery, in which case their punish-

ment would, I knew, be terrible, I resolved to go to
Falmouth and bring them away.

Having procured a pass into the military lines, I
arranged to start on a certain morning at daybreak.
The night preceding the day fixed for our departure—
for the Rev. Mr. Channing, now Chaplain to the House
of Representatives, had determined to accompany me—
witnessed the most terrible storm which I have ever seen.
It was about nine o'clock in the evening, and when the
storm was at its height, that I was seized with one of
those controlling impulses of which I had often read
but never myself felt before. I felt impelled to go that
night about five miles or more to the suburbs of Georgetown, to see an old Negro whom I had known in boyhood. Some vague impression that he could tell me
something to facilitate my search down in Virginia after
the contrabands may have mingled with this impulse ;
at any rate, so strong was it, that no protest from friends
or fury of the tempest could restrain me from going.
No hackman could be persuaded to go, and so I started
off through the storm and mud on foot. I arrived,
drenched, at my old Negro's shanty near midnight, and
found in his cellar the entire band of my father's Negroes,
who had arrived about ten minutes before me. Thus I
was saved the danger and expense of going down into
Stafford County.

They were a sad-looking set. Every rag on them
was wet. They looked as if they thought that Nature
had taken sides against them, and the elements turned
blood-hounds to pursue and yelp after them. Through
a long and weary way of about sixty miles they had
dragged themselves and their little ones, their beds and
chests. Each family had three or four young children,
and nearly every mother a babe at her breast. To me
they seemed a first arrival of Israelites, who had come

through the sea parted by the wand of God, their gar-
ments wet with its spray. Silent and gloomy they sat,
trying to hush their children to sleep or quiet. They
were all packed in one small cellar, over which the thun-
der crashed with alarming proximity.

Think how these poor people must have felt, launched
thus suddenly upon the great, and to them always un-
friendly, world! They knew not how near was the one
person out of the millions of the North who would take
any special interest in their fate. They had never known
a white face which was not that of a master. They had
never been beyond the little neighbourhood in which they
were born—had never seen cities, railways, steamers;—
these, with the whole North-land, were as much a vision
to them as the eternal fields arrayed in living green for
which they had so long sighed and sung. The terrible
storm, the natural misgiving as to the step they had
taken, the fearful doubt as to the destiny which awaited
them and their children,—all combined to make them
sit together and weep in silence.

Many years had parted me from them; but when I
entered, all knew me on the instant. The old woman
who had nursed me when I was a child sprang forward
and folded me in her arms as if I were still an infant.
They pressed around with their children, and clung to
me as to a lifeboat in their storm. Far into the night
we sat together; and they listened with glistening eyes
as I told them of the region to which I meant to take
them, where never should they

> " feel oppression,
> Never hear of war again."

But, for all the gladness of this night, my troubles
had scarcely begun. It was yet a question whether
Negroes situated like these were free to go to the North;

and Baltimore was yet a terrible Cerberus to Negroes
escaping from the South.   For every Negro taken over
them the railroads exacted bonds of £3000, with se-
curity, for fear they might be sued by some one for
taking off his slave.   And there was still a formidable
mob in Baltimore for any Abolitionist.   General Wads-
worth, then military governor of the district, was ready
to see me safely on the road to Baltimore, but could not
guarantee me transit through that city, which was under
Major-General Wool, a good but infirm old man, who
would never cut through red tape.   At Washington I
found that the mere mention of a Negro made the President nervous, and frightened some others of his Cabinet
much more.   The Negro has for a long time been the
touchstone of every man's courage in America, though
not so much now as then, when a formidable opposition
to the Administration was being organised on account of
its interference with Slavery.   Though my father was
a rebel, there was no machinery yet by which the title
of his slaves to freedom could be perfected.   As I was
going about from one to another trying to obtain authority to take these Negroes—between forty and fifty
in number—to the North-West, I felt something like
the minstrel who brought to King Arthur's court the
mantle which, because it would cover only the virtuous,
destroyed the reputations of so many fair ladies and
lords, and even that of Guinevere herself.   My dark
mantle shrivelled perceptibly on all, from the President
down, excepting one : Mr. Chase gave me such a letter
to General Wool as authorised him to grant me military
protection through Baltimore.   The exasperation of the
pro-Slavery mob of that city was so well known, that
many friends advised me not to try to take so many
Negroes through its streets to manumit them.   A con-
sultation was held at Senator Sumner's room, where an

officer suggested that the only safe mode would be to tie
the Negroes into a chain-gang, and, lash in hand, make
a show of driving them through the city; " in which
case," he declared, " all Baltimore will be on its knees
to you."

At last we started out from Washington, a large
concourse of people, chiefly contrabands, attending us.
But the terrors came upon us when we were set down
presently in the streets of Baltimore, with a small world
of baggage, and nearly three miles from the station from
which we had to start for Pennsylvania. There were no
arrangements to take any but white people from station
to station. As I have said, there were over forty of us,
and the sensation we made was immediate; we were
instantly surrounded by the hundreds of free Negroes
who live about the station at Baltimore, and who were
in a moment so mixed up with ours, especially the children, that I could not distinguish them; and, indeed, I
have since had an impression that Baltimore is chiefly
populated with Negro children under ten. For a moment there was danger that I should receive violence
at the hands of these Negroes; for there had been lately
many rumours of slaveholders hurrying their slaves out
of the District to Maryland, to evade the new Act of
Emancipation in the District. It was evident that the
crowd of Negroes thought that I was certainly the owner
of these contrabands, and perhaps was defrauding them
of their freedom; and they muttered and hissed around
me like so many black snakes, and impeded all my
efforts. But some signs passed from my contrabands to
them, which changed all this in an instant; the black
snakes disappeared, and in their places stood a large
number of cooperators, who in a brief space of time
had taken us, with our baggage, into wagons, and
were making with us a triumphal procession across the

city. But this procession was too triumphal for my
nerves; it excited attention in every street, and when
we alighted at the other station we had an ugly crowd
of low whites to encounter.

Alas, we had to wait here three mortal hours before
the train started! I took the Negroes into the regular
waiting-room, so completely had I forgotten the customs
of Slave States; of course the railroad-officials came and
drove us angrily out. I asked for *some* room; they had
" no room for niggers." I offered to pay for one, but
could not get it. I asked to be permitted to take them
into a carriage, but was told that the gate to the train
would not be unlocked for two hours. Meanwhile we
were in the street, and the crowd of low whites was increasing every moment; and they saw, by the delight of
the blacks, that it was an Abolition movement. Uglier
and uglier they became, glaring upon me, and annoying
the Negroes under my protection in every conceivable
way, until I could scarcely restrain the men from resist-
ing. I implored the Negroes to be patient, and pointed
out to the police the threatening aspect of affairs; but
they sneeringly said it was my own affair, not theirs, and
that I must take the consequences. Nevertheless, I had
a bit of paper in my pocket which would have brought
every bayonet in Baltimore to my aid, had it been
needed; and I declared that I was resolved to take the
Negroes through, though it should bring the guns of
Fort McHenry upon the city. Which very imposing
sentence, emphatically delivered, had an evident effect
upon the leaders of the crowd. Yet they persisted in
worrying the Negroes; and if I interfered, it was to be
cursed as " a d—d Abolitionist, who had brought on the
war."

At length, much to my relief, the ticket-agent appeared at his window. I saw that he was, as were the

other officers of the company, very angry at the presence
of the Negroes ; he was otherwise a fine-looking fellow.
He turned into a dark flint as I approached ; and when
I asked the price of tickets, he said angrily, " I can't
let those Negroes go on this road at any price." I knew,
of course, that he would have to let them go, but I knew
also that he could make things very uncomfortable for
me. I simply presented my military order to this very
disagreeable and handsome agent, and he began to read
it. He had read but two or three words of it, when he
looked up with astonishment, and said, " The paper says
these are your father's slaves ?" " They are," I replied.
" Why, sir, you could sell them in Baltimore for fifty
thousand dollars." " Possibly," I replied. Whereupon
(moved probably by supposing that I was making a
greater sacrifice than was the case) the young man's
face was unsheathed, and he said, " By God, you shall
have every car on this road, if you want it, and take the
Negroes where you please !" Then, having sold me the
tickets, he gave his ticket-selling to a subordinate, and
went out to secure us a car to ourselves ; and from that
moment, though the imprecations around us went on,
our way was made smooth.

It was about eight in the evening when we started,
and we were to travel all night. I observed that the
Negroes would neither talk nor sleep. They had put
their children to sleep, but were themselves holding a
silent watch. They were yet in a Slave State ; and
every railroad-station at which the train paused was a
possible danger to them. At last, when the name of a
certain wooding-up station was called out, I observed
that every eye danced, every tongue was loosened ; and
after some singing, they all dropped off to sleep. It
was not until next day that I learned that the station
which had wrought such a transformation upon them

was the dividing-line between the Slave and the Free States. How they knew it, I cannot divine; it was not even a village; but there the shadow of Slavery ended, and they knew or felt it.

The free and full conversations which I had with these Negroes were deeply interesting to me. They told me that, at the breaking out of the war, the Negroes all felt that their freedom was the issue. When they heard the guns of Bull-Run battle, it was only the extreme vigilance of their masters that kept the Negroes from running to join the Northern forces then; but this being the first test of their disposition, they were narrowly watched, and, finding that the hour of escape had not come, they put on the air of unusual quietness and loyalty, which had the (to them) very important effect of putting apprehension for the future to rest. When the Bull-Run battle was over, the majority of gentlemen went to the quarters of the Negroes, and told them— what they evidently believed—that the war between the North and South was over, and the South was victorious. Whereupon, such was the sinking of hope with the Negroes, that many of them were actually ill, and had to take to their beds. When they found that military preparations were continued, they were restored. Meanwhile their minds were systematically poisoned toward the North; they were told that the North would kill or sell them to foreign lands. For a time this was successful; but wherever our army went, this fear was cleared away. As for these Negroes of my father's, not one of whom could read or write, I found that they had a complete knowledge of all the stages through which the United-States Government had gone toward the recognition of their rights. The phase of the law at that time was, that every Negro who had been employed in any military service of the rebellion should be free; so each of these Negroes who had helped to lift a cannon, or set a stone, or dig at an entrenchment, had been careful to preserve the date and place where he did it, and the names of witnesses. They also knew the names of the generals who were friendly, and those who were un-friendly to them; and the name most venerated was that of John C. Fremont.

The faith of these simple souls in a Judgment-day drawing near has always been implicit. The days and nights, so serene to others, were to them fraught with portents of the approaching final adjudication between Heaven and Hell. Though the rumours and sounds of war had reached them, they had little realised what war was; and when at length the United-States army entered Falmouth, the Negroes one and all believed that the Judgment-day had arrived. The shells streaming across the river at the Confederates were to them its lightnings; the burning bridges of the Rappahannock, its flames; the white villagers rushing with shrieks to the woods were they who should call upon the rocks and mountains to hide them. (I give these interpretations literally as these Negroes related them.) In this belief, the Negroes gathered together in their kitchens and cabins, praying and singing their accustomed hymns; and wherever the soldiers entered, they found most of the houses empty, but in the Negro-quarters they found groups of Negroes on their knees. I could not help telling them that they had judged rightly,—that it was indeed the Day of Judgment for our guilty land; that His fan was in His hand, and He would thoroughly purge His floor, gathering the wheat into His garner, burning the chaff with unquenchable fire.

The Negroes were taken out to Yellow Springs, Ohio, where a house was prepared for their reception. At first some Irishmen threatened them, but the interest of

I

the community was so enlisted in their behalf that the Celtic population found it best to be quiet. Their labour was in immediate demand. They all found lucrative employment; and they have worked well enough to disprove the Southern slander, that their class will not work except under the lash. To this day I have heard no complaint of the idleness or misbehaviour of any of them. Some of them even offered to repay me what I had given for their transportation to the North-West, though they had so long laboured for my kindred and myself without remuneration. Their homes are now happy; their children are learning to read; their future is bright.

How many rescued families are there, of whom a similar narrative might now be told! These happened to have one to report the story of their passage through the sea to the land of Freedom, led by the fiery and cloudy pillar of War; but they have been followed by a host whose cry has been heard, and whose broken chain denotes the liberation of a nation which bore about its own neck the other end of that chain.

CHAPTER XIV.

The probabilities of Northern success—The classes of the
South—The poor whites—The new social stratum.

As the soldiers of the North go farther South, they will
find the population more and more definitely divided
into three classes: viz. the slaveholders, the slaves, and
the poor whites. Where there is a middle class of
whites,—of those, I mean, comparatively prosperous and
intelligent, but non-slaveholding,—there has always
been a powerful Union party, which has rendered the
advance of the Union forces less difficult; as witness
Western Virginia, Kentucky, East Tennessee, and Texas.
In conquering and occupying the South, then, the North
will have to deal with the three classes above named.
The number of those in regions as yet unconquered who
may be regarded as arrayed against the Union, are
about five millions, and a little over. This estimate includes, of course, the women and children, who are in
various ways an assistance to the rebellion. It includes
also nearly three millions of slaves, whose labour is a
support to the troops of the South, whether impressed
or not. It includes nearly two millions of poor whites,
who are blindly fighting against their own interests.
The number of slaveholders in the whole United States
was by the last census 348,000. The war has reduced
these by nearly 100,000. These are all who are really
and pecuniarily interested in the rebellion. As the
Union armies advance, the Negroes desert the South
in order to obtain freedom: their men become soldiers
for the North, and their women labourers in its camps.

Thus there is a continual diminution of men in the Southern armies, which, though sustained for a time by stretching the conscription from the age of sixteen to that of sixty, must at length fail for want of efficient numbers. Meanwhile the North gains in unanimity daily, as is proved by all the recent elections ; whilst the great accession of labourers by immigration enables it to pour increasing numbers into the South. Its success, therefore, is likely to be in the future what it has been in the past—slow but sure. It is easy for the as yet unvanquished to say that they will never yield, will burn their cities, and so on ; but those who remember that New Orleans, Memphis, and Vicksburg said the same as loudly as Richmond and Charleston up to the moment when they fell one by one into the hands of the United States, where they now lie with a quietness even unusual in the history of occupations,—will know how much credit to attach to such asseverations.

And this suggests the real questions, after all : Can the North hold the South after conquering it ? Will it not be getting a Poland ? If held successfully, will it not imply the substitution for a republic of a military despotism ? The sufficient answer to the first question is in the fact that the North *does* hold large portions of the South. even portions (as West Tennessee, Louisiana, Norfolk, Arkansas, and sections of Texas) where there was scarcely a vestige of any Union party. These she holds with garrisons of sixty per cent less force, in proportion to population, than those with which, in ordinary times, Francis Joseph holds Venice, or Napoleon holds Rome. The second and third questions can only at present be answered by our showing that the probabilities are strongly against the possibilities they suggest. If we suppose the slaveholders of the South in rebellion— not more than 250,000—and their families to be the

only class which will never remain quiet except under
coercion, it will at once be seen that in a nation of
34,000,000 they are not considerable enough to require
any great standing army to keep them in order. It
must be remembered, too, that the conquest of the South
involves the destruction of the slaveholding class by the
emancipation of their slaves, and, if they should not
accept the President's amnesty, the confiscation of their
estates ; for it has been deliberately decided by the
American people, that it is a first necessity that the
aristocracy of slavemongers shall be plucked up by the
roots.   For a time—possibly during the current generation—the hatred of this class may live, like the foliage
on a fallen tree ; but that which fed its life having been
withdrawn, the animosity can scarcely endure.   Slavery
withdrawn, these men and their children must get their
daily bread by free labour and under free institutions.
Men will adhere to, and if need be die for, that by which
they and their families live.   If Slavery is the basis of
their homes—if from slave institutions comes the bread
that sustains the wife and child—then they will fight and
die for Slavery.   If the home and the bread for wife
and child are derived from free institutions, then for
these will men fight and die.   Should the North be able
to compel the people of the South to get their daily
bread from freedom, they would soon be conservative of
freedom.   They would call the Yankees by many hard
names for some years after, doubtless, but there could be
no war between them ; on the contrary, every healing
influence in the universe would be at work to cure the
lacerations made by the tomahawk of Slavery, which
would then be buried.   Then every steamer, every train,
every telegraph - line plying between North and South,
would be a shuttle ceaselessly weaving together the hearts
of their millions into one woof of interest and affection.

The very intensity and virulence of the hatred which the South has for the North suggest that the feeling is extremely morbid, and not very deep. It is not deliberate, nor based upon any actual difference; and for this very reason must make up in violence what it lacks in the nature of things. The hate has sprung up too quickly to have much root or genuineness. It was within a comparatively recent period that the South was one with the North. They are of the same blood ; there is not nearly as much difference between them as between English, Scotch, Irish, and Welsh; their fathers were united within their memory ; and section has intermarried with section. France and England have become allies ; yet how long and bitter was the feud between them, reinforced by the formidable antagonism of race, which the one-sided hatred between the North and South is not! " I will fight a Frenchman," said Lord Nelson, " wherever I can find him ; wherever he can anchor, my ship shall be there." The people of the North and those of the South, in America, are of one blood; there has been but one satanic divider who has opened a chasm between them—Slavery. The interests of slavery cannot be made at one with the interests of free society ; there cannot be any legitimate institution of free society—as the free press, free speech, free school —which is not a bomb for Slavery. Free society being structurally and necessarily a continual assault upon Slavery, Slavery hates the North. As the Indian pleaded before the court, that not he, but the whisky killed the man, so we know well that it is not the Southern man, but the virus of Slavery in him, which hates the Northern man. I remember that during all the years of my deliberate advocacy of Slavery, I was filled with a cordial hatred of Northern men, not one of whom I had ever known ; but with the first step out of the atmosphere of

Slavery, with the first glance of doubt toward that institution, a cloud of illusions cleared up, my antipathy
to Northern men disappeared, and I felt a keen curiosity
and desire to see and know them.

But I have, perhaps, given more attention than is
necessary to the disposition which may be reasonably
hoped for in the educated (comparatively) and prosperous class in the South, as the result of better institutions. Even if so small a number should retain their
hatred to the bitter end, it would not matter so much,
if those who make up the Southern masses and labourers
should be reconciled. Now, I am not one of those who
believe in the existence of large numbers of Union men
in the states of the far South. I know very well that
the United States has occupied about all the-regions
where there was any important Union sentiment among
the people, with the exception of a central district of
North Carolina, where there has long been a strong
Quaker influence, and where the restoration of the Union
would, I know, be welcomed, though the Quakers will
not fight for it. In the eastern part of Virginia, and
in the States stretching around from North Carolina to
Louisiana, the only friends of the Union are the Negroes,
who are to play the most important part in the reformation of Southern society. The class, then, to be chiefly
considered is that of the poor whites.

Whilst I was engaged in preparing my pamphlet on
Free Schools in Virginia, I took the pains to visit the
districts inhabited by the poor whites; and for the two
years in which I was an itinerant Methodist preacher
under the Baltimore Conference, I had still more ample
opportunities for making myself practically acquainted
with their condition. I have thus learned enough to
convince me that this dumb, degraded, crushed class in
the Southern States is destined in the end to rest upon

the American mind more heavily than do the Negroes.
A volume might be written concerning them alone ; but
I will try and condense the leading facts of their condi-
tion into a brief chapter.

1. *Their numbers.* There is a popular impression that
the greatness and prosperity of a people is in some way
measurable by the increase of their numbers. But it is
the low and vile things—as frogs, flies, &c.—which spawn
most. In the lowest human races—those of the remote
East, for example—we find absolutely uncountable swarms
of people. The French statists have furnished many cu-
rious facts, which show that a general diffusion of wealth
and comfort secures that limitation of population which
many thinkers besides Malthus have thought most desir-
able. Toussenel says : "Ask the proprietors of the ponds
there; they will answer you that the ponds of Sologne are
so favourable to the growth of carp, that the rapid development of their size renders them barren ; and that in order
to preserve the breed, they are obliged to have ' ponds of
misery,' where they keep carp for reproduction. These
carp are baptised in Sologne with the significant name
of *peinards* — sufferers. Those households piled upon
each other in the narrow carperies of cities—those brats
swarming in the nether parts of every town—are human
peinards." The poor whites of the South confirm this.
They swarm. The old woman of the shoe is in every
hut of the South ; their floors are alive with bloomless,
squalid children.

2. *Social position.* They are really serfs of the soil,
without the advantages of serfs ; *orphaned serfs*, they
may be called. Having no square foot of the earth that
they can lease, much less own, they generally "squat"
down upon some landowner's estate, which the landowner is willing enough to permit; for no sooner does
the poor *peinard* fix himself there, than he is virtually

owned. The rich man can turn him and his family out of doors at any moment, or even imprison him for trespass, unless distinct permission to settle can be proved. These *peinards* may in some cases be sold. The formidable increase of the family makes the serfdom perpetual. They are worse off than the Negroes, being not so well dressed or fed ; hence there is a violent animosity between them, the Negro counting himself as far superior to " the poor white trash," which is his name for them, and which is the most offensive term which one Negro can cast at another. The two classes correspond to the labouring and the pauper classes elsewhere.

3. *Their occupation.* They are generally employed in doing nothing, and thereat are eminently successful. I have never been able to find how they earned even the pittance with which they get drunk, though sometimes they are employed to whip refractory slaves on farms, and their wives and daughters to sew clothing for slaves, and to cook the meals to be sent into the fields to the hands. Their greatest value to the rich slaveholding class is as *voters.* It must be remembered that there are only about as many slaveholders in the South as there are offices to be filled, and that each one, therefore, expects to be elected to some office; and he generally is so elected, chiefly by means of the votes of the poor whites whom he owns, in owning all by which they can live for another day.

4. *Their habits.* These are such as might shock even residents of London or New York. They drink perpetually that poison which they graphically term " rotgut whisky." In the region near Fredericksburg known as White Oak, I have gone from house to house, to the extent of over a dozen, and found in each the husband and wife, and in some cases the children, in a state of beastly intoxication. Rows and fights, in which the entire house-

hold and often the neighbours engage, are normal. On any Saturday afternoon there may be seen streaming out of any village in Virginia a long procession of two-wheeled carts, made of poles, with two or three old planks at the bottom, driverless or driven by some child, the horses being much more likely to fall dead than to run, the parents both stretched on the cart-floor dead drunk. Licentiousness of most loathsome forms prevails among them also.

5. Of course they have among them nothing that can be called religion or education. The nearest approach to these is, that sometimes a Methodist or Baptist meeting may be held near them—say, once or twice in three months. And to these meetings they add an hour of Sunday-school on each visit. In a collection of eighteen families, I found but one person who could read, and none that could write. The one who could read was a little girl of fourteen, who had acquired her accomplishment by walking to a monthly Sunday-school, through all weathers, five miles each way. She was much looked up to on account of her accomplishment. Indeed, I have found among these wretched people a deep consciousness of their degradation, and have seen hardy men weep that there was no prospect for their children but to grow up as ignorant and besotted as themselves.

I must declare, then, that, although I have visited with careful observation the Five Points of New York, and Whitechapel and Bethnal Green in London, I have never seen a population whose wretchedness, whether of soul or body, is so deep as that of the poor whites of the South—that class which Slavery has created by dis-honouring labour and abolishing wages, and which it has sunk lower with each year by keeping unproductive a third of the lands, whilst those who should be sustained by those lands are multiplied so fearfully.

I fancy that the war now raging in the South must have proved a step upward for the poor whites. That they would, one and all, enlist in it, was but the natural result of the few attractions presented by their homes, and their being told that the North was fighting to put them on a level with the " niggers." That they would fight well, would be natural to a people who find much of their subsistence by hunting, and are invariably good marksmen. That this war, by giving to those idle and rusty sinews and brains something to do, and imposing on them military restraints, may make it possible to bring a working class from them, seems to me very probable. I have heard already of some brave and hardy soldiers being promoted in the Southern army for their exploits, who came from the lowest class. Slavery alone can drag them down to their former degradation ; and that those very Negro-haters, the poor whites, will be found yet uniting with the North to prevent the re-establishment of Slavery, I am confident. The war has brought them into a position where their education is inevitable ; they will meet face to face and hand to hand the vigorous working-class of the North ; they will meet them as captors and prisoners ; and they will learn that, whilst they have had nothing but wretchedness and brutal ignorance at their homes, the lowest class of the North have comfortable homes and happiness and education ; they will learn what Freedom does for the people who enthrone her, and recognise what Slavery has done for themselves. At this moment nothing but their gross ignorance, the accumulated ignorance of generations, prevents the poor whites of the South from clasping as brothers and benefactors the men they are trying to slay, and turning their bayonets against the institution —destitution, rather—which, having sunk them lower than the slaves, now dares call on them to defend their own fetters.   Already in the States along the Mississippi, where the poor whites have come into contact with the Northern troops, this education has gone on to such an extent, that the military occupations which were declared impossible have, as we have seen, been unusually easy ; and organisations, by residents, for reunion with emancipation have sprung up where our armies have gone, without the encouragement of commanders or soldiers.

These, then, are the forces with which, and the elements upon which, the North will have to work in its task of bringing a new social stratum over the South which shall bury its saurian institutions, and make it fit to be the dwelling-place of a human society.   For a long time it may be reasonably anticipated that there will be thorns to choke the good seed, and rocks on which it will spring up to wither away.   But already there is a larger area of good ground where it will bear abundant fruit ; and that gradually the thorns will disappear and the rocks crumble into honest soil, is as certain as it is that the vitality of Liberty is greater than that of Slavery, and that the future belongs to Civilisation rather than to Barbarism.

Who can misread or doubt the prophecies written broadly over all the mountains, prairies, savannahs, lakes, and rivers of America?   What heart can have a misgiving that the superb grandeurs and resources of that continent have been prepared for a race of slaves and slave-drivers?   Are the nine hundred thousand square miles of rich lands of the South, and the mountain-ranges veined with iron and gold, to culminate in slave-shambles?   Every hill-top in America is a Pisgah from which can be seen the promised land of Liberty, which that nation is sure, soon or late, to enter.   Already in Virginia, North Carolina, South Carolina, Tennessee, Mississippi, Louisiana, Texas, Arkansas, the types of the new man and the new society which are to reign in them have appeared ; and though at present their foot-hold is small and precarious, they are the signs of a revolution that can never go backward. The small stone hewn from the mountain-top will fill the whole land of the South. The planter will see that at Beaufort and Port Royal free-labour gets twice as much cotton from the acre as slave-labour ever did. The poor whites will see that where schools and libraries and the dignity of labour prevail, the spell under which they have been so long dwarfed is broken. And to the poor Negro the banner of the Union, which hitherto has seemed to symbolise the stripes on his back, shall float up to be what it was meant by the fathers to signify, —the morning-stars and streaks of a new dawn for Humanity.

CHAPTER XV.

An Address to the English people.

THERE is a modern philosophy which aims to supersede the ancient belief in a Judgment-day. Every day, it declares, is a judgment-day: the evil or good thing, or man, is damned or imparadised on the instant of its conception, and in virtue of its being good or ill. Very important, certainly, is the truth contained in this statement; yet we can scarcely credit it with an insight so deep as that which is discoverable in the more universal presentiment of a great day in the future, wherein final adjudication is to be made between Heaven and Hell, Right and Wrong. *Iddio non paga il Sabato.* Though Justice is ever awake, her thunders sleep long; or rather, we may say, things do mature to their good or evil consummation—the last petal organically unfolded from the true being immortality; the last from the evil, death.

The strata of the earth, each burying a past dynasty and transmitting the heir of the higher which advances, anticipate the epochs of History, or the authentic separations between social forms unworthy to reign longer, and those which can be the adequate trunk and members for the Spirit of the Age. Of course each epoch has its own day of doom; but the succession of revolutions cannot end until the Highest is enthroned and the Lowest chained in the pit. " Justice," said a Persian sage, " is so dear to the heart of Nature, that if at the last day a single atom of injustice were found, the Universe would shrivel like a snake's skin to cast it off for ever."

Not without meaning, also, was that ancient in-

stinct which prophesied of the consummation of all
things by fire. How universal is the susceptibility to
combustion ! Rub two sticks together, rub any metal,
strike any pebble, and you rouse the consuming element that sleeps in each until the hour in which it
must work its change. This element, the child and
restless devotee of the sun, purifier and destroyer, from
the earliest period impressed the heart of the world
as the agent of the final decree. Fire is the symbol
of both Love and Wrath,—much closer allies than
they seem to be. When Love is mightiest, it cannot
indulge ; it smites and scathes. " Love," said Maho-
met, " is the Hell-spark that burneth up the Mountain of Iniquity." Standing before the fierce confla-
gration of War and Agitation sweeping through the
world to-day, the Past with its wrongs shrivelling like
a burnt scroll before it, the listening ear can hear a
voice from the burning which tells of a Supreme Love,
which thus saves man from his own darkness and evil,
at whatever cost. There is, it whispers, no cold marble
of indifference to human action and human destiny at
the heart of the Universe, but a great core of fire whose
flames kindle at once the demon's torment and the se-
raph's rapture, whose love is at once the flame of Hell
and the glow of Heaven. Too much Love reigns in
this world for man to be suffered to go on in Wrong
safely and serenely.

In the light of these principles, to which each day
brings some new ray of illustration, we may read in the
signs of the present time portents such as have always
marked the sealing-up of outworn epochs : there are wars
and rumours of wars in every land ; and nations and
races are " linked each to each by woes of fiery change."
The war-storm passing round the planet is to-day hurled
in one thunderous surge against the walls of Western

Europe ; and if these walls, daily growing weaker, shall
yield, the world will be girt with an unbroken sea of
dissolving fire.   Even the dull ear may now hear

> " Time flowing in the middle of the night,
> And all things *rushing* to a day of doom."

" A mad world, my masters !"   Yes ; but there is
a vast deal of method in its madness.   Not the most
peaceful tree that grows to-day is more systematically
developed through the Protean forms of a leaf, than are
these revolutions.   From the first faint dawn of Christianity, which has created an insurrection in China,
to the war in the New World, which is clearing the
path for its highest triumph, these revolutions are strung
on one thread.   History will reckon this as the epoch of
disintegration ; but we must be content, remembering
that the first work of every awakening germ of life is
that of disintegration : over the ruins of the seed-shell,
beating down the sod under its feet, the germ arises to
its glory.   There is no cant among the germ-cells, that
the seed-shell must not be broken until there is a flower
or fruit all ready to be put in its place.   The germ,
having done its duty of destruction, trusts itself to the
powers of air, light, and rain, which stand ready to
give it its full shape and fruit in due season.   Liberty
is always the life-germ of Humanity, and its first sign
of activity in any epoch is the destruction of the old
forms, which no sooner cease to represent than they
begin to trammel it.

Liberty, as against established forms, is so normally
the principle of revolutions in the Old World, that it has
become here almost axiomatic, that revolutionists are
always in the right.   The Southern Confederacy and its
champions in England seek boldly to take advantage of
this foregone popular judgment, and are eager to gain a

verdict by identifying their case with that of the Poles. Of course neither of these would have the same high opinion of revolution if it were the slaves of the South or the people of Ireland who were engaged in it. The truth is, that the axiom of the righteousness of revolutions is no axiom at all. In a good government, a revolution would be the highest crime. A band of robbers is as revolutionary as the Polish army; the only difference is, that the former are organised for a bad, the latter for a good object. Revolution, if not for better and juster laws, is mere lawlessness. All justification of the Southern rebellion, as being after the precedent of the revolution of the American colonies against George III., is simple nonsense, unless it can be shown that the colonists rebelled in order to establish laws less just and institutions more barbarous than those fastened upon them by the mother country.

For almost the first time in history, the world sees a revolution going on wherein the revolutionists are striving for the cause of injustice and oppression, and the established Government for, or at least in the direction of, liberty and equality. When Earl Russell was asked in the House of Lords why England, which had so often interfered in behalf of peoples seeking their independence, should not now interfere in behalf of the Southern Confederacy, he replied, that "when England had interfered in such conflicts, it had always been in the interest of human freedom, and he trusted that she would not now begin to mar that record." This answer rested upon a strange new fact, and one whose analysis would reveal the entire difference between the Old World and the New. Let us examine this fact more closely.

The French have summed up all progress in their watchwords—LIBERTY, EQUALITY, FRATERNITY. These are the three rungs of the ladder by which Humanity

K

ascends. First comes Liberty, which is another name for life itself. This the mole burrowing the sod and Garibaldi clearing the path of freer empires equally seek. Men must be free to fill out the outlines of their own being, else they cannot be said, properly speaking, to exist at all; they are but ciphers multiplying the life of some imperial unit at their head. But independence may be directed to evil as well as good purposes, since, as we have seen, every brigand is independent. Also, independence ending in itself is worthless, as would be the blade of corn which, having revolutionised the sod, should go no further toward bearing its ear. Hence it is the law of health that Liberty must flower into that which is higher than itself,—namely, Equality. Yet as the blossom of a plant is only a higher form of its leaf, Equality is the higher form of Liberty; it being found that men are so interwoven in their interests, that not one can be truly free unless all others have their freedom also. And yet further is it true, that as the fruit is only a higher form of the blossom, and consequently of the leaf, so Equality must rise to Fraternity—the ultimate form of Liberty and the destiny of man. That is, as it has been found that men are so related that the enslavement of one impairs the liberty of all, — from which springs the demand for equality,—so no one can, alone and without sympathy, develop his full nature, which is the only real freedom. It needs all to make each. "One man is no man." A man to be really free must not only be liberated from the domination of other men, but from his own limitations; from those last gratings he must be freed, by freely giving where he is strong and receiving where he is weak. And this is Fraternity —the fruit in which Liberty, if it is not abortive, must culminate.

Now the Old World is on the first rung of this lad-

der. It is still in the thick of the battle for mere Liberty;
and hence every heroic virtue gathers about those who
are striking off the shackles of the mind and body. The
value of freedom, the fitness of men for it, the right of
men to support only Churches in which they believe, and
to be represented by the Governments they must sustain,
—these are vital questions in the Old World. But these
are not vital questions in the New. On that fresh page
of the world which God has turned, the very preface was
Liberty. That nation began at a point which the Old
World is just reaching. When the Declaration of Independence was signed, the battles of the New World for
Liberty were closed for ever. There is no difference
between any two men on that continent about Liberty :
all love and believe in it. There is not a slave-driver in
the South who does not desire Liberty. The South is
fighting for Liberty as much as the North,—the one for
Liberty to bind others, the other for Liberty to be just.

The best summing up of the principle involved in the
American War that I have heard was from the lips of
a Yorkshire mechanic at Leeds lately. We had heard
a plausible address from a cultivated gentleman, its
object being to show that the South had the same right
to its independence that the American colonies had to
theirs. At the close of it, the dusty mechanic got up on
his chair and said : " I have something to say. I have
no doubt that the Southerners are plucky fellows, nor
that they are fighting for their liberty; but the fault I
find is, *they are not willing to share it*. When they are
willing to give to their labouring people the liberty they
wish for themselves, they may justly come here and
ask us labouring people for our sympathy—not before."
Then he sat down, amid the hearty applause which he
deserved. This was the real *Ilias in nuce*. The war
raging in America must be referred to a higher plane

than that of Liberty. It is a war for Equality. It is to decide whether the Liberty which each race claims for itself, and knows to be good, shall be given impartially to all, of whatever colour or degree. Judged with reference to that standard of Equality,—or the right of each to do and be his best, under God, without human hindrance,—which is higher than mere Liberty, it will be seen at once that the Abolitionists are the real revolutionists, and that the defenders of the old-established wrong are those who are claiming to be the Poles of America. And the established Government, which is assailed only because it was being peacefully revolutionised by the friends of justice, has a right to all the sympathy which naturally flows out from noble hearts to those who are giving their lives and treasure to redress a deep wrong.

I know that I have assumed that Slavery is the one issue in the civil war in America. It seems almost insulting to the popular intelligence of England not to assume it. Yet it appears that there are in England— not in America, North or South—those who allege other reasons for the war. Men living in a country where English and Scotch dwell quietly together, tell us that the war arises out of constitutional differences between the people! Men who belong to an empire on which the sun never sets, tell us that the American nation has broken up on account of its size! And we are told that the South seceded and fired upon the Union because of a tariff, as if it were not nobler to revolutionise from a fanatical devotion to even a bad institution, than to plunge millions into years of bloodshed and devastation simply on a question of money! As a Southerner, I protest against this last theory, as painting them blacker than they are. The Southerners are at least outspoken, and South Carolina is to be believed when she declares, in her secession ordinance, that she left the Union because she believed the institution of Slavery to be threatened. Jefferson Davis is to be believed when he declared, in the speech with which he left the United-States Senate, that the South had not any "pecuniary" motive in seceding. The Vice-President is to be believed when he asserts that their object is to establish a new empire, whose corner-stone is Slavery.

As to the motives of the North in prosecuting the war, they are of no importance, when it is remembered that the North, in going South, can only carry what institutions it has, and that these are free institutions. To suppose that the armies of the Union have, as their sole object, the emancipation of slaves, is to suppose a country behind them too far advanced ever to have had a war about Slavery. If Civilisation should abandon all that Selfishness has achieved—is achieving—the strongest institutions would crumble. The only important question is, Are their victories necessarily victories for freedom? Does the slave pray for a sight of their banner? It almost seems to me that only the wilfully blind can fail to see Liberty and Justice hovering over the army of the Union, so palpable are their signs. If ever a nation gave out evidences of a national regeneration, faithfully going on, it would seem that the American Union has so done within the last few years. From the very spot where one of the first anti-Slavery martyrs fell—Lovejoy, of Illinois—comes Abraham Lincoln, elected on the anniversary of his death, to represent at the capital the nation's direction, at least, toward the principles for which he died. In the United-States armoury, where John Brown and his companions hurled themselves against Slavery, to their death, to rescue its victims, troops of liberated slaves bear the arms of the Government which are to save their brothers yet bound.

The only surviving son of John Brown instructs freed
men at Arlington, Virginia; his daughter instructs them
in South Carolina. The shambles of many a Southern
town are now filled with ammunition for the war against
the oppressors of the weak and defenceless. The arms
of the Union captured John Brown, and gave him to
the gallows in Virginia; the last anniversary of his death
(December 2d) was celebrated at Washington by the
lifting of the great statue of Liberty to the top of the dome
of the new Capitol. Where General Lee, within sight of
that Capitol, was, four years ago, surrounded by his slaves,
at Arlington, a town of freed Negroes, with schools and
churches of their own, now stands; whilst Lee is contriv-
ing how he may prevent similar ones from being planted
throughout the South. The plantation of Jeff. Davis is
now a camp of Negro soldiers of the Union. Where, a
few years ago, Daniel Webster, of Massachusetts, stood
in the United-States Senate to urge the passage of the
odious Fugitive-Slave Bill, which Mason of Virginia had
demanded of the North, a senator of Virginia now
stands, to urge the passage of its repeal, as demanded of
the country by the senator who replaced Daniel Webster — Charles Sumner. When to this is added the
freedom of every territory of the Union — the actual
liberation of nearly a million slaves — and the pledge
given, which the people have resolved shall never be
recalled, of freedom to be given to all whom our soldiers
may reach—it would seem to be a very strained point
that the North is not fighting for freedom. Though a
few men like Banks still try to disgrace the cause and
betray it, though the President himself falters, one can
scarcely think that any of us, having a parent or child
enslaved in South Carolina to-day, would sympathise
with the Confederate armies, or be very anxious to have
the war cease at once. And is it not remarkable that

in Canada, the United States, and England, not one *Negro* has yet appeared against the cause of the North? I, for one, would take the opinion of a Negro on the American war sooner than that of any white man. If a man is set free, the motive of those who set him free, whether selfish or not, is of very little importance to *him*.

Now, men and women of England! a few closing words to you, and I have done.

American Slavery is just now speaking for itself so loudly,—inaugurating and waging a cruel civil war, and covering a fair land with desolation, on the mere question of its title to an infinite expansion and perpetuity, —that one might have hoped that nowhere beyond the poison of its own atmosphere, least of all in England, would there be any place for further testimonies and discussions concerning that institution. And yet, now when Slavery has thrown off every disguise, has revealed every fang and claw, nay, has shown that it has arms long enough to reach across the ocean and snatch the bread from the English working-man's table, we find in England a public opinion weakened and divided concerning it, and some of the ablest thinkers either indifferent to its ravages, or ready to lay the blame of them at every door other than that to which it belongs.

This is the most painful sign of the present time. The English mind impresses itself more deeply than that of any other country upon the character of all nations which pretend to civilisation at the present day. No more forcible illustration of this, as far as America is concerned, need be given, than the anti-Slavery movement in that country, which took its watchwords from England; watchwords to which every thinker, orator, and poet rallied, urging them until the conscience of the nation was aroused, and Slavery was forced—for this

rebellion was not at all unnecessary if Slavery wished to
live — to have recourse to the only arguments it had;
to wit, the bowie-knife and musket.

It is not my purpose to seek out the causes of this
departure from the old standards; but I do wish to remind you, that the evil results of it have been and must
be serious and practical.   And for these reasons:

We can scarcely, in this age of the world, look to
the sword for the accomplishment of any clean and complete reform.   At the same time, remembering the wick-
edness of the assault of the South upon the Union, and
that it was under the inspiration of divinely-implanted
instincts that the people of the North arose and abandoned the peaceful occupations which they loved for a
conflict with those to whom they bore no hatred, and
one in which the North must itself suffer a pang for
each it inflicted,—we must see this war as one which
was written on the iron leaf of Fate, and therefore may
reasonably hope that it will bring about those modified
conditions upon which the higher forces, that can alone
lead on any perfect reform, can act.

There can be no doubt that there are resources in
the heart and brain of the world, were they fully drawn
upon, sufficient for the settlement of all those questions
which, by their default, are now generally thrown back
to find their adjustment amid the convulsions of Chaos
and the fires of the Pit.   And this default is chiefly in
the lack of concentration and purpose on the part of the
moral forces.   The power of a perfect alliance, the weak-
ness of an imperfect alliance, have many familiar illus-
trations in recent European history.   Who does not
know that Russia would cease from her bloody crimes
against Poland to-morrow if she knew to-day that there
was a *perfect* alliance between the Western Powers in
their determination to prevent them?   And who can doubt

that if the indignant protest of every nation, and of every author, orator, press, and pulpit, of Europe and the Northern States, had been combined and hurled in one thunderstroke against Slavery in the South, it would have withered up under it? But a divided opinion else-where implies a united opinion where Slavery is an immediate interest. The present attitude of Slavery is the direct result of the absence of any thing like a united conviction in civilised countries against it. We are possibly too fast in pronouncing Slavery to be against the Spirit of the Age : that will be decided by the American War, for nothing can resist the Spirit of an Age ; the evil it confronts melts like an iceberg at the tropics. There was a time when there was a united *sentiment* in Christendom against Slavery ; the leading men of all countries, including those of the South, freely assented and admitted that Slavery was wrong. It was in large part, however, only a sentiment,—many of them holding slaves whilst they denounced Slavery,—and of course could not do the work of a conviction ; but we may see in that which a united sentiment could sketch, what a united conviction could realise. At the time to which I allude, Slavery in America consented freely to its decline, and had no dream of life, much less of extension and empire. But one day it managed to clutch one of the most important of the world's purse-strings, and thence-forth there arose a party rich enough to buy for it a Science, a Literature, and a Gospel. Then Slavery leapt from its death-bed, provided its feast, and was received into good society : it sat in its judicial seats, with the ermine on its brow ; it sat in the President's chair ; it entered the pulpit, and for it the Bible was clasped with handcuffs, and the very cross of Christ festooned with chains.

L

Against this frightful usurpation the anti-Slavery men, though few and often faint, inaugurated a revolution. Spared at first because of their insignificance, they at length, through much suffering, have raised their cause to a sufficient equality with Slavery to bring on those tempests which, as Lord Bacon says, may in the calendars of states be looked for when things come to an equality, as in the natural world they attend the equinoctia. That when the storms are past Freedom will be uppermost, they do not doubt : nevertheless the world will not enjoy a more magnificent triumph than it is equal to. And moreover, this idea of Equality, of which the Negro is a mere temporary representative, is so world-wide and human, that we have a feeling that the Humanity of the world is to be drawn upon to demand and see to it, that the chains of the American slave are so completely broken and swept away, that never again, so long as the world lasts, shall a man try to enslave his fellow-man.

Knowing that there is much work to be done yet, the anti-Slavery heart of America is anxiously asking : Whilst the forces of nature are seething and working to bring about new conditions in America, is there a corresponding activity in the spiritual forces of Christendom, leading to a power competent to deal with those new conditions ? When the iron is withdrawn from the furnace, will the brain and heart of the civilised world be there with a conviction strong enough to strike and fashion it to the measure of justice ?

Great God, that this should be a question in England to-day !—that it should be something to canvass whether her poets and preachers, her scholars and statesmen, can be surely counted upon as opposed to having men and women sold like cattle, and children torn from their mothers' breasts by vile men for gain! Yet, blush as we may for our common race to say it, there is a very serious doubt as to how many of the most influential men of England, if asked to-day to unite in a protest against the existence of Slavery for one moment longer, would utter some cant or fatuity about the bad results of emancipation in the West Indies, or the unfitness of the slaves for freedom (which is about as wise as to talk of the unfitness of an invalid for health). At any rate, if the leading minds were united on this thing, and standing where they should be, in the vanguard, we should not now be taking shame upon the Anglo-Saxon race by recording, that in the year 1864 it was still a question not easily answered about this or that leading man, whether he was for emancipation or not—whether on the side of the wolf, or of the babe it is seeking to devour!

In a military sense, you, men and women of England, are and should be neutral; but in the moral question involved in this conflict neutrality were a crime. The freedom of four millions of slaves, the redemption of a race,—these are such victories as all may share in, of whatever land; and if we fail to win them, it will be because our common race is unworthy of, and unequal to, a great achievement in any direction higher than the heaping up of gold.

In the Day that is approaching there can be no neutrality: each must take his part, to the right or the left. Well will it be with him who recognises under all colours the great march of human destiny; who under all can recognise where is beating that one heart of Humanity whose pulses are supplied from the heart of God, whose laws it infallibly executes. For the end is not yet. These struggles for Liberty in the Old World will but deliver it to the conflict for Equality. When the strong wind that rends the mountain of Despotism is past, the fires must come which shall consume all thrones and castes that preserve unreal distinctions. How great the need that the hearts of all true and just men shall be knit together for that day! O brothers, it is by standing together, amid the trials of such conflicts, that we are trained for the grander day, when wars shall cease— when, after the wind and the fire, shall come the still small voice, that shall lead Liberty and Equality to their full glory in Human Fraternity.

THE END.

.

For EU product safety concerns, contact us at Calle de José Abascal, 56–1°, 28003 Madrid, Spain or eugpsr@cambridge.org.

www.ingramcontent.com/pod-product-compliance
Ingram Content Group UK Ltd.
Pitfield, Milton Keynes, MK11 3LW, UK
UKHW012339130625
459647UK00009B/402